909.828 HEAT

D1349389

REMEMBER THE 80s

This edition first published in the UK in 2006
by Green Umbrella Publishing

Printed and bound in Italy

ISBN: 1-905009-66-6
ISBN-13: 978-1-905009-66-4

REMEMBER
THE
80s

Edited by Michael Heatley

Written by Peter Gamble, Mike Gent, Ian Welch and Claire Welch

CONTENTS

REMEMBER THE EIGHTIES

1989 1988 1987 1986 1985 1984 1983 1982 1981 1980

1980

FASHION, CULTURE & ENTERTAINMENT

Steve McQueen dies

Movie Legend Steve McQueen died a premature death at the age of 50 on 7 November 1980 from a rare and painful form of lung cancer. Born on 21 March 1930 in Beech Grove, Indiana, McQueen never knew his father and was brought up by his uncle in Missouri, where he was left by his mother, until the age of 12 when he moved with her to Los Angeles. Two years later his

mother sent him to a reformatory school. He left school and joined the US Marine Corps in 1947. Five years later he began acting lessons with the financial support of the GI Bill (the US Bill of Rights or Serviceman's Readjustment Act which provided college or vocational training for GIs).

Having triumphed over a poor education and a broken home, McQueen went on to become one of the most prolific movie actors of all time. He was one of the most sought-after superstars in the world with his tanned and rugged good looks and lived his life to the full both on and off screen.

Despite his success as an actor he considered giving it up to follow his other true passion – racing. He was experienced with both motorbikes and cars on the professional circuit. These talents gave him the ability to perform his own driving stunts in movies. Luckily he committed himself to the big screen

Above and below: Steve McQueen shortly before his death and in a scene from the film 'Bullitt'.

and films such as *The Great Escape, The Sand Pebbles, Nevada Smith, Bullitt, Papillon* and *The Getaway* are all considered classics by film critics and fans alike. It was *The Magnificent Seven*, in 1960, which launched his film career and made him a superstar.

McQueen possessed a captivating on-screen persona and was known for being difficult to work with and his dislike of directors and producers is well documented.

In 1997, modern technology put him at the steering wheel of a Ford Puma in a TV commercial, driving around to the *Bullitt* soundtrack.

Kickers/stonewashed/stretch jeans

Chunky, colourful Kickers from Belgium, with their little flower-shaped leather logo attached to the laces, caused chaos in 1980. Manufacturers couldn't make them quickly enough and they were so popular that shoe shops stayed open until late in the evenings waiting for delivery.

They were not just for the young and trendy; older generations were snapping up Kickers too. Kickers are owned and licensed by the Pentland Group plc, who also own some of the world's best-known shoe and sporting goods brands. For its first 50 years the group was an obscure manufacturer, but under the helm of chairman R S Rubin the company reached a global platform in the early 1980s.

At the same time as Kickers were walking out of every shoe shop in the country, stretch jeans and stonewashed fabrics became extremely popular. Jeans originally came from a material made in Europe and probably got their name from the sailors from Genoa, in Italy, who wore clothes made from this material. The word denim originated at the same time from a particular French material from Nimes, called serge de Nimes, which was a durable twill-woven cotton fabric with traditionally blue warp and white filling threads. In 1853, Leob Strauss began a wholesale business, later changing his name to Levi. But it was the 1930s Westerns on the big screen that gave jeans their popularity.

By 1980, stone-washed jeans – first created by François Girbaud – were popular, following the pre-washed look from designer Jack Spence for Lee. The effect was created by using pea gravel, then pumice which floated around with the jeans rather than lying at

Below: Kickers boot.

1980 1981 1982 1983 1984 1985 1986 1987 1988 19

Rubik's Cube

Originally called the Magic Cube, the Rubik's Cube was re-manufactured, renamed and launched in May 1980. It is known to be the world's biggest-selling toy and there have been over 300 million sales of the Cube and its imitations sold worldwide.

Erno Rubik, a Hungarian sculptor and professor of architecture, invented the Magic Cube in 1974. It is a mechanical puzzle made of plastic, shaped in a cube which is available in four different versions: the 2x2x2 or pocket cube; the 3x3x3 and the 4x4x4, known as 'Rubik's Revenge'; or the 5x5x5, called the 'Professor's Cube'. The 3x3x3 cube was the most popular and is made of 27 unit cubes. Faces of each cube are covered by stickers which come in six colours, the object of the puzzle being to make each side of the cube a solid colour. In 2005, to celebrate the twenty-fifth anniversary of Rubik's cube, a special edition with a central sticker reading 'Rubik's Cube 1980-2005', was released in a presentation box.

the bottom of the wash. Turkish stones were preferred for their porous qualities along with stones from Sicily, but supply for these is, even today, limited.

Also around this time, denim mixed with other fabrics became the norm and polyamide, lycra – creating the stretch effect – and polypropylene or polyester were used along with a 100 per cent nylon net which has special bonding effects, creating a more active look. The trends that became so popular in the early 1980s continue today with two-way stretch fabrics, special coatings and rubberised effects.

Above: Men's fashion in 1980.
Below: The Rubik's Cube in action.

REMEMBER THE EIGHTIES

Pacman

Pacman (also known as Puckman) was first released in 1980 and was an extremely popular arcade game. Developed by Namco and licensed by Midway, it is universally considered one of the classics and landmarks of all arcade games and was synonymous with video games during the 1980s. An icon of the decade's popular culture it was a non-violent game which appealed to all ages.

The game was developed by Toru Iwatani, who devised a maze game where players move the Pacman (a yellow circle with a mouth) to navigate the maze while 'eating' small dots and other items. The player moves up a level when all dots and items are eaten. However, the player must also out-manoeuvre the four ghosts, Blinky, Pinky,

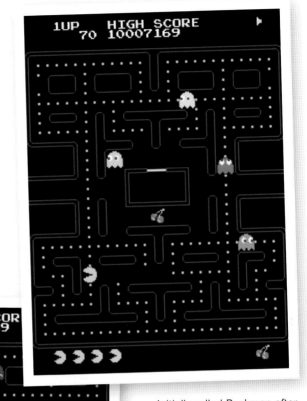

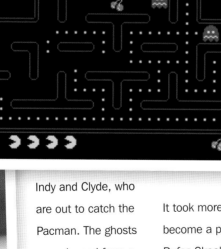

Indy and Clyde, who are out to catch the Pacman. The ghosts are released from a 'ghost pen' one by one at the start of each level.

Initially called Puckman after the Japanese for 'he eats, he eats', the game received a lukewarm reception in Japan where games such as Space Invaders were more popular. However, release in the US resulted in a worldwide phenomenon within the video game industry and the style of game-play became widely imitated by competitors.

Fruit of the Loom

It took more than 100 years for Fruit of the Loom to become a popular style of clothing. The daughter of Rufas Skeel, a cotton merchant, designed the logo (which remains unchanged to this day) in 1851 to draw attention to her father's clothes in his shop in Providence, Rhode Island.

Above and below: The very addictive video arcade game 'Pacman'.

1980 1981 1982 1983 1984 1985 1986 1987 1988 1989

The fruit paintings were then used as a trademark by cloth maker Robert Knight who thought the designs were perfect for his trade name 'Fruit of the Loom'. The distinct apple, grapes, currants and leaves logo is ranked one of the most recognisable trademarks worldwide. Knight received a patent number (418) for the brand in 1871, just one year after trade laws were passed by Congress.

In 1980, the collections featured classic and contemporary styling combined with comfortable cotton fabrics which were available in many shops. The company was, and still is, committed to its customers and as a vertically integrated manufacturer controls the quality of garments from start to finish. Fruit of the Loom manufactures its own yarn, knit and cloth. It cuts and sews the fabrics as well as packaging the clothes for sale.

MUSIC

March

The Jam's burgeoning popularity was evident this month when their tenth single, 'Going Underground' (a double A side with 'Dreams of Children') went straight in at Number 1; a newsworthy feat, last achieved by Slade six years previously. Advance orders looked to be sufficient for the single to debut at the top but record company Polydor made no mistake, issuing the first 100,000 copies as a double pack with a three-track live EP and releasing it on a Tuesday, rather than the usual Friday, allowing a full week of sales to register.

The Jam were midway through an American tour which was swiftly truncated to allow them to return home in time to appear on *Top of the Pops*. To celebrate, frontman Paul Weller inexplicably wore a Heinz Tomato Ketchup apron inside out. The band had three further chart-toppers, including, in December 1982, their final single 'Beat Surrender'.

August

The premiere of the feature film *Breaking Glass* in London took moviegoers back to the punk movement of just a few years earlier. Starring bleach-blonde singer/actress Hazel O'Connor, it depicted the rapid rise to fame and equally swift fall from grace of her punk band, and provided rather grittier viewing than the equally popular *Fame*. She picked up a BAFTA nomination, and was the first female to both star in a hit film and write/perform its soundtrack.

Producer Tony Visconti of David Bowie/Marc Bolan fame had lent his backing to the project, and also

Above: The Jam – Paul Weller, Rick Buckler and Bruce Foxton perform on stage.

played bass on the resulting album which spawned the hit singles 'Eighth Day' (en route to Number 5 this very month) and 'Will You?' Ironically, O'Connor's own career would be blighted by management and record-label disputes in echoes of her trouble-torn character and she would never eclipse this first celluloid success despite a later one-woman show titled *Beyond Broken Glass*.

September

The year that would come to a shocking close with the murder of John Lennon had already witnessed the passing of several other musicians. During the night

1980 1981 1982 1983 1984 1985 1986 1987 1988 1989

Below: Hazel O'Connor in a scene from the film 'Breaking Glass'.

worsening epileptic condition caused Curtis to take his own life.

A heroin overdose killed Malcolm Owen vocalist of the Ruts, best known for their punk/reggae fusion and the single 'Babylon's Burning'. Following his death in July, the others in the band continued for two more albums as Ruts DC.

of 24 September 1980 Led Zeppelin drummer John 'Bonzo' Bonham choked on his own vomit after a prodigious drinking spree. The tragedy effectively ended Zeppelin's career. The remaining members issued a press statement which said: 'We wish it to be known that the loss of our dear friend and the deep respect we have for his family together with the sense of undivided harmony felt by ourselves and our manager, have led us to decide that we could not continue as we were.'

In the early hours of 19 February, lead singer of Australian hard rockers AC/DC Bon (Ronald Belford) Scott was found dead in a friend's car in London. Like Bonham, Scott had been imbibing heavily; the cause of death was recorded as 'acute alcoholic poisoning'. He was replaced by Brian Johnson, former vocalist with British glam-era outfit Geordie.

Joy Division, an influential post-punk quartet from Manchester, looked to be on the verge of major success with their second album 'Closer' ready for release and an American tour imminent when singer Ian Curtis hung himself at home on 18 May. Depression and a

In October, Steve Peregrine Took, part of the original Tyrannosaurus Rex with Marc Bolan, died after choking on a cherry stone whilst in a haze after taking drugs. Following his dismissal from the duo in 1969, the former Stephen Porter had only enjoyed peripheral involvement with music.

Above: AC/DC.
Below: Led Zeppelin drummer John Bonham.

1980

REMEMBER THE EIGHTIES

Rock with men resplendent in foppish finery, from kilts and velvet breeches to frilly shirts and make-up. David Bowie was regarded as the godfather of New Romantic; the video for his 1980 single 'Ashes to Ashes' featured up-and-coming figures like Steve Strange of Visage.

A different strand of the movement arose

November

The latest youth cult to emerge in Britain was New Romantic. Its early standard-bearers were Spandau Ballet, a London quintet who released their debut single 'To Cut

A Long Story Short' in November.

The trend, which emerged in London clubs Billy's and Blitz, sported a look reminiscent of Glam

simultaneously in Birmingham's Rum Runner club where Duran Duran, Spandau Ballet's major rivals, were the house band. Duran keyboardist Nick Rhodes compared the two scenes. 'People were going out to enjoy themselves in Birmingham. In London people went out to pose in a corner and scowl at people who didn't have the right haberdashery.'

Above and below: Spandau Ballet and arch rivals Duran Duran.
***Below left:** Steve Strange (right) of the New Romantic group Visage.*

1980 1981 1982 1983 1984 1985 1986 1987 1988 1989

1980 1981 1982 1983 1984 1985 1986 1987 1988 1989

December

The assassination of John Lennon on 8 December sent shock waves not only through the music business but around the world. The 40-year-old ex-Beatle had spent the last five years out of the public eye, preferring to spend his time bringing up son Sean, and had just released his comeback album 'Double Fantasy', recorded with wife Yoko Ono.

John's decision to devote himself to family life rather than work had seen him take advantage of his relative anonymity to go on long walks with Sean round Central Park, visiting the circus and taking holidays. Musical activities would have to wait 'until we feel we can take time off...maybe when Sean is about three or four.'

The man who brought him back to music was mogul David Geffen who, having discovered the Eagles among other groups, had now founded his own label. Five years of silence had ended in November with the release of 'Double Fantasy', its songs reflecting a new philosophy, while the single '(Just Like) Starting Over' was John's first hit for six and a half years.

Lennon had rediscovered his urge to make music, and the world awaited his next move with interest. Sadly, the wait would be a long one. John and Yoko

Below: Crowds gather outside the Dakota building after the news of John Lennon's death.

tragic news spread like wildfire, crowds of grieving New Yorkers gathered outside the Dakota in the darkness. Three thousand miles away in John's home town of Liverpool, fans held a silent vigil which would be repeated by millions worldwide on 14 December at the request of Yoko Ono. The record-buying public reacted by buying his records in numbers unprecedented since the 1960s, and three different singles, '(Just Like) Starting Over', 'Imagine' and 'Woman', would hit Number 1 in the UK in just seven weeks.

SPORT

Five times Borg

Bjorn Borg, the Swede with the ice cold temperament, captured his fifth consecutive Wimbledon singles title in July when he defeated the immensely talented but volatile John McEnroe in a four hour five-setter which captivated the crowd.

were approaching the Dakota building after a day at the recording studio when they were accosted by Mark Chapman, an unknown 25-year-old security guard from Hawaii to whom Lennon had given his autograph earlier in the day. He was obsessed with Lennon and had, it appeared, been stalking the Liverpudlian for three days before shooting him five times at point-blank range.

Lennon was rushed to Roosevelt Memorial Hospital, but was pronounced dead half an hour after arrival. As the

Above: Mark Chapman, the convicted assassin of John Lennon.
Below: John McEnroe in action against Bjorn Borg in their epic Wimbledon Men's final.

1980 1981 1982 1983 1984 1985 1986 1987 1988 19

despite his Wimbledon victories he was never able to dominate the tournament quite like the great Swede.

Moscow Olympic Games

Despite the absence of Kenya, West Germany and USA, who held a boycott, the Moscow Olympics proved to be a remarkable success.

Many feared that, with three major medal-winning nations avoiding the

McEnroe took the first set 6-1, suggesting an upset was on the cards but Borg battled back to take the next two, before relinquishing number four in a tie-break. Set up for the perfect finale, the Swede eventually won the battle of wills to come out the 8-6 winner in the last set.

Borg had set out to write himself into the record books and be regarded as one of the greatest ever players. With this, his final Wimbledon victory, he had certainly done that.

The following year, McEnroe reversed the result and for the next few years he became the man to beat. But

games, competition would suffer somewhat but once the events were under way all worries were proved unfounded.

Britain produced some outstanding gold medal winners if not that many.

On the track Steve Ovett and Sebastian Coe both raced to glory in the 800 metres and 1500 metres

Above: Borg celebrates his victory for a fifth year.
Below: Ovett pulls ahead of Coe to win the Olympic Games 800m.

LEARNING RESOURCE CENTRE

1980 1981 1982 1983 1984 1985 1986 1987 1988 1989

The charming Nadia Comaneci returned to the Olympic stage and took two gold medals but had to give way to the tiny Russian star Yelena Davydova for the all-round individual title. The team title went to the home nation.

Certain sports as always were dominated by individual countries; for example the

respectively, Allan Wells took the 100 metres and Daley Thompson became the first Briton to win an Olympic decathlon.

Wells came close to achieving the sprint double but was just edged out by the Italian Pietro Mennea in the 200 metres. Elsewhere on the track the man who became known as 'Yifter The Shifter', Miruts Yifter, did the 5,000 and 10,000 metres double for Ethiopia.

In the pool, the distinctive bald-headed Duncan Goodhew struck gold for Britain in the 100 metres breaststroke and Sharron Davies produced a 400 metres individual medley silver. For the most part the swimming events were dominated by the Eastern bloc as were the women's gymnastics.

boxing had a distinctive Cuban flavour as only one of the eleven weights failed to have a medallist from the land of Castro. The Cubans took six golds, topped off by Teofilio Stevenson, who for the third successive games took the heavyweight crown. On the water, the German Democratic Republic took every gold medal bar one for the men's rowing.

Above: British swimmers Duncan Goodhew and David Wilkie.
Below: Daley Thompson celebrates his gold medal in Moscow.

1980 1981 1982 1983 1984 1985 1986 1987 1988 1989

Muhammad Ali's return

Boxing folklore says great fighters should never come back, and the great Muhammad Ali proved that this holds good for even the finest exponents of the noble art.

Ali had become a much loved figure around the globe as, over a lengthy career, he had turned his sometime calculated youthful brashness into a knowing maturity which had seen him through some increasingly testing times in the ring as the years moved on. He was undoubtedly 'The Greatest' but had started to take a few too many punches before his retirement in 1981.

Many fighters have been tempted back into the ring for various reasons, often financial, sometimes because of ego, frequently due to not being able to live without that adrenalin rush they get when entering the ring.

Whatever Ali's reasons, they were ill-conceived for he appeared just a shadow of his former self.

In October, at the age of 38, he got into the ring with Larry Holmes, a very good fighter who would have given Ali a run for his money when the ex-champion was at his peak. Needless to say, timing and fleetness of foot were consigned to history as Ali stumbled his way as far as the tenth round before the referee stopped the fight. One can imagine that Holmes got little satisfaction from the victory.

As if to compound the aberration, Ali did not hang up his gloves permanently after the fight, for the following year he took on Trevor Berbick in the Bahamas only to taste defeat once again. Berbick was the kind of opponent who would have given Ali little trouble ten years earlier.

Below: Muhammad Ali gives a press conference before his fight with Larry Holmes in Las Vegas.

in the public's eye, Gierek fell from grace, under the guise of having heart problems, to be replaced by Stanislaw Kania, the man in charge of security matters.

Kania's background indicated that tolerance towards the workers might not stretch too far; this was actually proven the following year, but via a different party.

In December 1981, General Jaruzelski, regarded as a moderate, brought in martial law to quell continuing unrest. Over 14.000 trade union members were arrested including Lech Walesa, troops could be found at all the major points of real or potential dissent and fighting broke out between workers and security forces. The Silesian coalfields were the scene for bitter clashes that left seven dead and the Gdansk shipyards turned into a battlefield which left 300 people injured. The next month

There is no sadder sight than watching a once great sportsman plying his trade like an also ran, and Ali was no exception.

POLITICS & CURRENT AFFAIRS

Solidarity

After an apparent easing of the authoritarian regime, Polish shipyard workers formed an organisation called Solidarity in September. This was a trade union movement that had sprung out of the crippling strikes which had brought concessions from the Edward Gierek government. The Gdansk shipyard worker Lech Walesa took the role of movement leader, and as his star rose

Above: Friends and relatives listen to Lech Walesa (centre) outside the gates of the Lenin shipyard in Gdansk, Poland.
Below: Walesa in trade unionist pose.

food riots broke out with Gdansk at the centre of the protest, although later in the year Walesa was set free.

Noises were made by Jaruzelski, that although he had taken harsh measures, in the long run the people of Poland would benefit from the government's new policy. Communist party officials were not immune to the cleaning up process, as a number found themselves in the dock for crimes against the state, the highest profile individual being the disgraced Gierek.

The fallout from the Polish unrest had spread to virtually every other Eastern bloc country by the end of the decade.

SAS storm Iranian Embassy

In a real life drama played out on national television, an elite force of Special Air Service personnel, stormed the Iranian Embassy in Knightsbridge on 5 May to end a stand-off that had existed for nearly a week.

A group of gunmen had been demanding the release of political prisoners in Iran and had taken a number of hostages within the building to back up their demands.

Above and below: SAS commandos storm the Iranian Embassy.

Once they had started killing their captives (the body of the press attaché had been thrown outside onto the steps) and threatened to kill others, the SAS had no alternative but to take dramatic action. Firstly, television viewers could see an explosion on the first floor, then flames leaping from the building. A BBC employee who had been caught up in the situation emerged from within, much to the surprise of the SAS men on the balcony. Another explosion boomed out and gunfire punctuated the normally genteel surroundings. At the rear of the building more personnel abseiled from the roof and burst through the windows.

The story that emerged from the inside, included an heroic act from PC Trevor Lock who had been on duty at the time of the hostage taking.

He had managed to secrete his revolver and at the moment the SAS attack commenced he grappled with the terrorist leader, allowing the Special Forces to kill the man before he had time to do any further damage.

In just over ten minutes, four of the five gunmen were dead and 19 hostages led to safety. Unfortunately, an Iranian diplomat lost his life, and another was badly wounded, when the terrorists started shooting at the first signs of SAS action.

Due to the sheer professionalism of the Special Forces, loss of life had been kept to a minimum and proved how necessary such a unit is.

Ronald Reagan wins the presidency

Outside of the USA, the idea of a jobbing ex-actor making it to the top of the political tree is very unlikely but in November 1980 the impossible happened. Ronald Reagan, former governor of California, was voted into the White House.

The troubled Carter administration, which had battled with problems ranging from the Iran hostage crisis to major energy problems, finally succumbed at the ballot box. The public had been unhappy with the regime for some considerable time and rewarded Reagan with a landslide victory.

The Carter/Mondale ticket was blown away by the Republican pairing of Reagan and George Bush, with the final figures making uncomfortable reading for Democrat supporters. Reagan won all but 6 of the 50 states, the voting being 43.9 million to 35.4 million. Carter also carried the ignominy of being the first presiding president to be beaten since Herbert Hoover in 1932.

1980 1981 1982 1983 1984 1985 1986 1987 1988 1989

Above: Ronald Reagan at his ranch in California shortly before his inauguration as president.

1981

1980 1981 1982 1983 1984 1985 1986 1987 1988 1989

FASHION, CULTURE & ENTERTAINMENT

Cats opens

Based on Old Possum's *Book Of Practical Cats* by TS Eliot with music from Andrew Lloyd Webber, *Cats* opened at the New London Theatre on 11 May 1981. The show ran for exactly 21 years, closing its doors on 11 May 2002 after its 8,949th performance, and was the longest running musical in British history. The original cast members included Elaine Paige, Brian Blessed, Paul Nicholas, Wayne Sleep, Sarah Brightman and Bonnie Langford. The very first performance was interrupted by a bomb scare (common across London at the time) and the theatre had to be evacuated.

Cats became the catalyst for Andrew Lloyd Webber and Cameron Mackintosh who revolutionised the musical genre. Their productions have dominated stages worldwide for more than 20 years. On 12 May 1989, *Cats* became the longest running musical in London's West End when it performed its 3,358th show and on Broadway when it overtook *A Chorus Line's* record of 6,137 performances during the 1990s. More than eight million people in London, and 50 million worldwide have seen the musical which took in excess of $2 billion. It was performed in 26 countries, more than 300 cities and was staged in 11 different languages.

Directed by Trevor Nunn with associate direction by Gillian Lynne, the show was designed by John Napier with lighting design by David Hersey. It was produced by Cameron Mackintosh and the Really Useful Theatre Company Limited. On the show's last night on 11 May 2002 a live video relay of the last show was broadcast to a giant screen in Covent Garden's Piazza at 8.30 p.m. Original cast members were present to greet fans on the Piazza while 150 former cast members attended the show at the New London Theatre.

New Romantic fashion

ABC, Visage, Spandau Ballet, Soft Cell, Simple Minds, the Human League, Thompson Twins, Depeche Mode, Adam and the Ants and Duran Duran, to name but a few, were all artists and bands said to belong to a musical

Above: Some of the cast from 'Cats'.

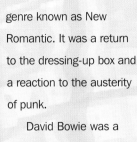

1981

genre known as New Romantic. It was a return to the dressing-up box and a reaction to the austerity of punk.

David Bowie was a huge influence both in the music and the fashion that became New Romantic. His 1980 hit 'Fashion' was considered as the 'anthem' for New Romantics. It started, mainly in the UK, at the beginning of the decade in London clubs such as Billy's (which ran Bowie nights). Billy's eventually became the Blitz Club, a highly successful and elite club which featured Steve Strange as doorman and Boy George as a cloakroom attendant. The idea gave rise to many hundreds of New Romantic clubs in and around London including: the Regency, Chadwell Heath (where Culture Club and Depeche Mode had debut gigs) and Croc's in Rayleigh in Essex.

The phenomenon was similar in many ways to that of 1970s glam rock. However, instead of guitar rock, synthesizers and electropop along with rhythm machines, became synonymous with the music. Bands like Ultravox (of 'Vienna' fame) jumped on the bandwagon to good effect.

Unlike the punk era, New Romantics made an effort to look flamboyant in an almost narcissistic way, and adapted factual or fictional themes and Hollywood glamour to create a personal look. It was colourful and

Below left: Marc Almond of Soft Cell.
Below: Thompson Twins.

1981

the British high street. The expansion of Hepworth over 50 years resulted in a nationwide retail chain of men's clothing which led to the company going public in 1948. By the late 1970s however it was suffering from its conservative image and chairman Terence Conran decided that the company needed to reinvent itself.

In 1981, Hepworth bought Kendalls, another retail chain with 80 locations which catered to the women's wear market. The acquisition also saw a new chief executive, George Davies, who was given the job of reinventing the two chains as one. Davies set about branding the merchandise under the new name Next and all stores were based in former Kendalls shops.

The first year brought turnover of more than £82 million and by the end of 1982, nearly all 80 Kendalls stores had been redesigned to the Next concept.

The French Lieutenant's Woman

With a screenplay by Harold Pinter and directed by Karel Reisz, *The French Lieutenant's Woman* is cleverly portrayed as a film within a film from the novel by John Fowles of the same name. It starred Meryl Streep as Sara, the woman whose reputation is ruined by her torrid affair with a French sailor in the sexual and social oppresion of the Victorian era and Jeremy Irons as

dramatic with frills and glamorous fabrics (often associated with historical periods). Pioneering early designers of the Romantic look included Vivienne Westwood, who made adaptions of Regency designs which were intended to look dandy, David Holah, Stevie Stewart and Colin Swift.

Next

For more than a century from its origins as J Hepworth & Son founded in 1864 in Leeds, Next plc (formed in 1981) has been clothing the UK and is a mainstay of

Above: New Romantics in London's King's Road.

REMEMBER THE EIGHTIES

Charles, the quintessential Englishman who becomes obsessed by her. Streep and Irons also played the 1970s actors making the film, Anna and Mike, whose affair off-screen mirrored the characters they are portraying in *The French Lieutenant's Woman*.

With music from Carl Davis and supporting cast roles from Jean Faulds, Lynsey Baxter (who plays Ermistina – Charles's love interest) and Hilton MacRae as Sam, the film spends its time divided between two stories with increasing similarities.

Streep won the LA Film Critics' Association award for Best Actress in 1981, and was nominated for an Oscar – she also won a Golden Globe for Best Actress in the same year. The film also won three BAFTA awards for Best Actress (Streep), Best Sound and the Anthony Asquith Award for Original Film Music.

Pixie Boots and the return of occasion wear

Pixie Boots were a huge phenomenon in 1981. It was every young girl's dream to own a pair. Usually made from suede in black or brown, they were short ankle-length boots with a flat heel that were easy to pull on. The material around the ankle was wrinkly and,

Above: Jeremy Irons with an award for 'The French Lieutenant's Woman' alongside actress Dee Hepburn.
Below: A scene from the film 'The French Lieutenant's Woman'.

1980 **1981** 1982 1983 1984 1985 1986 1987 1988 1989

although styles developed and changed during the early 1980s, the mainstay of the fashion remained for a long time. Pixie Boots were influenced by the styles of shoes worn by male New Romantics with a mix of swashbuckling pirate styles popular at the time.

The flamboyant edge of New Romantic fashion also brought back a desire for occasion wear that had been pushed out during the counter culture of the 1960s early 1970s and by the punk era from the mid-1970s onwards. Glamour became the norm in the early 1980s and occasion wear was influenced by the romantic idea

of dressing up. Lace, oversized collars, cocktail dresses and slinky satin clothes once again found popularity.

MUSIC

February

Phil Collins launched an amazingly successful solo career this month with the release of his debut album 'Face Value'. Collins joined Genesis in 1970, stepping out somewhat reluctantly from behind the drum kit to take on lead vocal duties six years later following the departure of Peter Gabriel. With Collins at the helm, the band gradually moved away from the complex, progressive rock of their early albums towards a more radio-friendly style.

'Face Value', the lyrics of which centred on the singer's recent divorce,

Above: Phil Collins pictured with Kate Bush and fellow Genesis band-mate Mike Rutherford.
Below: Collins in concert.

both 'Face Value' and the group effort 'Abacab' topped the British chart. He succeeded in running the two high profile careers in tandem, even finding time for some acting roles, until 1996 when he finally left Genesis.

May

The world mourned the passing of Bob Marley, Reggae's first superstar, who lost his battle with cancer on 11 May 1981, aged 36. He was honoured with a state funeral in his native Jamaica.

The singer had survived an attempt on his life in 1976 when a gunman opened fire on Marley, his wife, Rita, and his manager. Bob escaped with minor injuries to his arm and chest.

The following year, a wound found on his right big toe, at first thought to be a football injury, was revealed to be cancerous. In accordance with the Rastafarian belief that the body must remain whole, Marley refused amputation. Whilst touring America in 1980, the disease was found to have spread. He flew to Munich

was an immediate hit on both sides of the Atlantic and the first in a series of commercial triumphs which saw Collins sell over 100 million albums worldwide. In 1981

Below: Bob Marley.

for treatment but the cancer was terminal. En route to spend his final days in Jamaica, Marley was too ill to travel beyond Miami, where he died in hospital.

July

The Specials' 'Ghost Town' spent three weeks at Number 1 in July 1981 as riots raged in Britain's major cities. Composed by keyboard player Jerry Dammers, the song seemed to encapsulate the mood of the country with lyrics referring to Britain's high unemployment rate and crumbling infrastructure. The band, however, were not convinced about the connection.

'All that topicality stuff can get a bit phoney. I'm not sure about it all really,' was lead singer Terry Hall's verdict. 'Ok, there were riots and they needed an anthem I guess, but I didn't connect it at all.' Dammers concurred. 'I wasn't trying to write an anthem, it was just a protest song.'

'Ghost Town' was to prove the Specials' swansong. At the end of 1981, internal tensions caused the band to split. Hall, guitarist Lynval Golding and vocalist Neville Staple formed Fun Boy Three whilst Dammers went on to lead the Special AKA.

September

Adam and the Ants were a punk band who toyed with bondage imagery and had made one largely overlooked album before Adam (real name Stuart Goddard) sought career advice from Malcolm McLaren, former Sex Pistols manager. McLaren suggested a change in

1981

Below: The Brixton riots which were believed to be the inspiration for the Specials' 'Ghost Town'.

disbanded the Ants to go solo in March 1982. When his popularity began to wane, Adam branched into acting.

December

Synth pop went mainstream in 1981, climaxing with the Human League's reign at Number 1 over Christmas with 'Don't You Want Me'. The parent album 'Dare' was also a massive seller. Like Adam and the Ants, the Human League achieved enormous success in unlikely circumstances. The original band were critically lauded but commercially unsuccessful and their reputation for dour art rock was turned on its head when two founder members left to form

musical direction and the adoption of a new look which mixed Red Indian and piratical elements. When the Ants defected to McLaren in early 1980 to form Bow Wow Wow, the future looked bleak for Adam but he assembled a new group, whose lynchpin was guitarist and co-songwriter Marco Pirroni. By the year's end, they had notched up two top ten hits.

With a sound influenced by African Burundi drumming and constantly changing visuals, Adam became the pin-up of 1981. September's chart topper 'Prince Charming' was his second Number 1 of the year. He

Heaven 17 and spectacularly-fringed vocalist Phil Oakey recruited two girl singers he met in a Sheffield club.

Ultravox were another outfit who achieved success after losing a founder member. After three albums, the final one of which embraced synth rock, singer John

Above: Adam and the Ants.
Below: Malcolm McLaren.

1980 **1981** 1982 1983 1984 1985 1986 1987 1988 1989

REMEMBER THE EIGHTIES

adherents of punk's DIY philosophy. The work of German futurists Kraftwerk and David Bowie's 'Low' and 'Heroes' were set texts for up and coming synthesiser bands. Gary Numan's sci-fi take on synthesiser-driven pop proved the commercial possibilities of a genre which was often viewed with hostility by traditionalists who questioned its authenticity.

Foxx left to go solo and in came the well-travelled Midge Ure. Early in 1981,'Vienna', the band's first major hit single, notoriously spent four weeks at number two, three of them behind Joe Dolce Music Theatre's novelty record 'Shaddap You Face'.

In the summer of 1981, electronic duo Soft Cell had provided one of the year's most memorable hits with 'Tainted Love', a cover of the Northern Soul classic originally performed by Gloria Jones, who became Marc Bolan's partner. At the same time, Depeche Mode broke through; the best-known song of their early poppy incarnation was 'Just Can't Get Enough'.

The synthesiser had been used in rock music since the late Sixties but it was not until the end of the 1970s that the instrument became both affordable and practical, giving it an obvious appeal to

Above: Ultravox.
Above right: Influence on both the music and fashion of the era, David Bowie.
Below: Kraftwerk, the godfathers of synth.

SPORT

Champion and Aldaniti win the Grand National

Amidst scenes of great emotion rarely seen at horseracing events Aldaniti ridden by Bob Champion claimed the Grand National in April. The story behind the pairing read like a film script and eventually would find its way onto celluloid with John Hurt taking the central role. The pairing really had no right to be seen on a racecourse, as both parties had a history of illness and injury.

Champion, one of the country's leading jump jockeys had been diagnosed with testicular cancer in 1979, being given only eight months to live at one stage despite intensive chemotherapy treatment. He had manfully fought against the diagnosis and came to the 1981 National as a thirty-two year old still in remission. The previous eight unsuccessful Nationals he had ridden in never deterred him from the belief that one day the race would be his.

Aldaniti's career on the other hand had been constantly dogged by injury, in fact as a sickly foal vets had come close to putting him down. Against his better judgement, trainer Josh Gifford had bought the horse in 1974.

Years of patience followed as the animal suffered recurring tendon trouble and most seriously a broken hock bone. Consequently, when the duo arrived at the start of the National nobody could guess exactly how they would perform, although they were one of the more fancied combinations.

Champion allowed Aldaniti to sit comfortably in the pack for most of the first circuit but lead throughout the second, a feat in itself. The scenes of jubilation as horse and rider passed through the finishing line were unparalleled.

A year later the jockey had retired due to weight problems and took up the reins as a trainer. The ensuing years saw the setting up of the Bob Champion Cancer Trust and the opening of a research unit at the Royal Marsden hospital in Surrey under the Champion name.

Below: Bob Champion with Aldaniti.

Botham's magical Ashes series

Ian Botham's efforts in the cause of English cricket are something of legend, much of it based on the remarkable events during the Ashes series in 1981. The opening Test had been won by Australia at Trent Bridge by four wickets with the second at Lord's being drawn. The captaincy was not sitting easily on Botham's shoulders and after a pair of ducks at Lord's he gave way to Mike Brearley for the Headingley Test. In one of the most amazing turn arounds in cricketing history 'Beefy' and Co. turned a seemingly hopeless position into a famous victory.

England were following on and when Botham walked out to bat still needed 92 runs to avoid an innings defeat with only three wickets remaining. In an awesome display of controlled hitting the all-rounder scored an unbeaten 149, leaving the tourists a very gettable 130 to win.

Even after Botham's battling feat few fans could have expected anything less than an honourable defeat but a fired-up Bob Willis took 8 for 43, leaving the Aussies bowled out for 111.

So England entered the fourth Test at Edgbaston with the series all square at 1-1 and once again the

Below: Ian Botham smiles as he hits six.

1981

Britons swap mile record

The domination of Britain's athletes over the mile and 1500 metres was illustrated in the space of 10 days in August when Sebastian Coe and Steve Ovett took it in turns to break the world mile record.

Ovett's exisiting record had stood for a year until Coe, the only man likely to challenge it, started chipping away at it with a run in Zurich, where he reduced the time by 0.3 seconds.

Two days later Coe set the seal on this phenomenal sequence when before 40,000 delirious spectators at the Heysel Stadium in Brussels he clocked 3 minutes 47.53 seconds which would stand as the record until Steve Cram came along and smashed it four years later.

Heady days which may never be repeated.

game turned into a personal triumph for Botham.

The Australians needed just 46 runs to win with five wickets in hand when the all-rounder took the ball for a final spell. Twenty-eight balls later he had claimed all five wickets for only one run and secured yet another England victory.

The Ashes were eventually retained at Old Trafford, as Botham scored 118 in England's second innings, his hundred coming off only 86 balls. The target of 506 proved too much for the visitors, despite the captain Allan Border hitting 123 not out whilst nursing a broken finger. The match was won by 103 runs giving England a 3-1 margin which they took to the inconsequential drawn Oval test.

Above: Botham the 'all-rounder' bowling for England.
Below: Sebastian Coe in action.

1980 1981 1982 1983 1984 1985 1986 1987 1988 1989

POLITICS &
CURRENT AFFAIRS

US hostages released

January witnessed the release of the US hostages who had been held in captivity for a total of 444 days. As they landed in Algiers, the 50 men and 2 women appeared tired but overjoyed at the end of their ordeal. Across America, every town and city produced a cacophony to herald the release of their countrymen.

Originally, they'd been taken at the end of 1979, when a mob attacked the US Embassy in Tehran and rounded up over 70 people. The attack had been seen as retribution for the outgoing Shah being allowed entry into the US to seek medical attention and fuelled by the anti-American stance of the Iranian spiritual leader Ayatollah Khomeini whose hard-line regime had not long been in power. Although a few hostages had been released over a period of time, the majority had remained incarcerated, occasionally paraded on Iranian TV to taunt the US and often suffering torture.

The Jimmy Carter regime had been under constant pressure to 'get them back home' by any means but as very little or no diplomatic activity took place between the two countries, it was left to individuals from other parts of the world to attempt to broker a deal. Carter had imposed oil sanctions on Iran but this had led to a further worsening of relations.

More than one rescue mission had been planned in typical US fashion.

The first, designated Operation Eagle Claw, had come close to lift-off but, after a series of mishaps, ended with the deaths of eight US servicemen. The second lay dead in the water after hitting problems at an American desert location. Patience became the watchword.

The hostage release may have been a relief for so many but did nothing for the relationship between the

US and Iran. At the start of the twenty-first century the two countries appeared further apart than ever.

Shooting of the Pope

In May, the unthinkable happened when Pope John Paul II was shot and wounded in St Peter's Square. The Pope had been taking a drive through the crowds in an open-top jeep, a weekly event where he blessed the assembled throng, when a gunman struck, wounding both the pontiff and two women. This being a regular event, the would-be assassin had only to wait his chance in a situation where the victim would always be vulnerable. The Pope's security people must have always feared such a situation and their nightmares had come true.

Above: US hostages on their return from Iran after being held captive for 444 days.

The Pope was rushed to a nearby hospital where an emergency operation took place to remove four bullets, two of which were in his lower intestine. Eventually, an announcement came from the hospital that the operation had been successful and, despite the extent of his injuries, the Pope should recover in time. He had a reputation as a resilient individual who had survived the ravages that the Nazis had inflicted on his native Poland and on this occasion he would come through again.

The gunman, a Turkish national by the name of Mehmet Ali Agca, had meanwhile been arrested by the police, after a gun had been wrested from him. It turned out that he was known to the Turkish police as an extremist to watch and Interpol had a record of his details. He had entered Italy under false papers, posing as a student, and had arrived in Rome with the intention of killing the Pope in a strangely misguided attempt to bring the world's attention to the USSR's

1980 1981 1982 1983 1984 1985 1986 1987 1988 1989

Below: Bodyguards hold Pope John Paul II after he was shot in St Peter's Square.

crimes in Afghanistan and the US's similar actions in El Salvador.

Some years later the Pope came face to face with his would-be assassin in a moment of reconciliation and forgiveness.

The marriage of Charles and Diana

The marriage of the Prince of Wales to Lady Diana Spencer took place at St Paul's cathedral on 29 July, singling it out as both the royal and social event of the year.

Millions around the world watched on TV and thousands thronged the streets as the popular prince plighted his troth to the seemingly perfect and beautiful young Diana. In a euphoric atmosphere the Archbishop of Canterbury, Dr Robert Runcie, carried out the ceremony to unite one of the country's most respected families with 'the Firm', as the Duke of Edinburgh calls the Royal Family.

1981

The couple left the cathedral to be greeted by ecstatic crowds, who lined the streets all the way to Buckingham Palace. After the wedding breakfast they appeared in time-honoured fashion on

Below: David and Elizabeth Emanuel who designed Diana's wedding dress.

the Palace balcony and the cheers grew louder when the couple shared their first public kiss. The crowds were still in place when the Prince and Princess emerged to drive off on their honeymoon.

For one, brief, shining moment, it looked like a marriage made in heaven.

Above and below: Charles and Diana wave to the crowds from their carriage and the Palace balcony.

1982

FASHION, CULTURE & ENTERTAINMENT

The Barbican opens

Known for being Europe's foremost multi-arts and conference centre, the Barbican was officially opened by the Queen on 3 March 1982. Today it still promotes a year-round programme of music, film, art and education. Owned, funded and managed by the City of London (the third largest sponsor of arts in the UK), the Barbican was designed during the 1960s.

Construction of the site took place during the 1970s, at a phenomenal cost of £161 million. The seven-acre site also houses the Guildhall School of Music and Drama and the Barbican Library – both of which are under separate management. Described by the Queen as one of the wonders of the modern world, it was built as the City of London's gift to the nation in order to promote the arts.

The Barbican is open all year-round and presents a diverse array of activities including classic and contemporary music, international theatre and dance, visual arts, design and film programmes that promote both first-time films and themed seasons. More than 27 million visitors have attended more than 52,000 events since the doors opened. During each year, the Barbican receives a substantial grant from the City of London as well as making its own direct income of more than £12 million.

Contained within the site is a concert hall which can be adapted for conferences with seating for more than 2,000, two theatres, three cinemas which seat a total of 688 and 4,645 square metres of foyer and public spaces. There are two art galleries, comprising

the Barbican Art Gallery and the Curve, a lakeside terrace and a roof-top conservatory which houses tropical plants and flowers. Also included are seven conference suites, two trade exhibition halls and private

Above: The Barbican plays host to a sheepdog display.

REMEMBER THE EIGHTIES

Hairstyles

Influenced by a variety of trends, from Joanna Lumley's 'Purdey' cut in the popular TV series The *Avengers* (1976-79) to big hair copied from soaps like *Dallas* and *Dynasty*, women's hairstyles during the 1980s were generally emphasized in volume and size. The style reflected society's concern with wealth and influence and it seemed that just about everyone had 'big' hair.

While even today voluptuous hairstyles are sported in some quarters, it was the 1980s where hair made more of a fashion statement than in most decades before or since. Power suits and music culture contributed greatly to the influences surrounding hairstyles. New Wave music also contributed to styling with the rise in short, asymmetrical haircuts. Despite similar cuts and lengths, with clever use of products and hairdryers, the remarkable variations available in hairstyling were immense. Elements of 1980s hairstyles can still be seen today in asymmetrical cuts, romantic curls and high-volume waves.

The Purdey haircut was simply a slick bob, combed forward, which had a definite back neckline contour. Versions of this were evident throughout the 1980s and even the late Princess of Wales sported

function rooms. The three restaurants also housed within the site include the Waterside Café, the Balcony Bistro and the formal Searcy's restaurant.

39

Above: Farrah Fawcett displays her 'big' hair.
Below: Toyah Wilcox with her large hair.

1980 1981 **1982** 1983 1984 1985 1986 1987 1988 1989

1980 1981 **1982** 1983 1984 1985 1986 1987 1988 1989

a version of the cut in her engagement photos in 1981. Other hairstyles were influenced by the earlier punk styles of the late 1970s and proved very popular nationwide. Even people with short hair had big hair and working women often opted for slightly toned-down styles that could be easily blow-dried or worked with an electric styling brush.

The previously popular Carmen-style heated rollers and hair rollers disappeared from homes up and down the country as blow-drying and shaping strands of hair over the face firmly established the way that women preferred to style their hair and flicks became more popular the bigger the hair became. New products like mousse and hair gel were widely available and once *Dynasty* appeared on TV screens the tousled, windswept look demanding strands and lots of work to achieve it became the norm.

During the early 1980s another very popular style for both men and women was the afro perm. Naturally curly hair and permed hair were quite dominant throughout the 1980s. Wax became another firm favourite for styling hair, while gels contributed to the popular wet look.

Ra-ra skirts, headbands and legwarmers

Young girls everywhere wanted to own a ra-ra skirt. Short, above the knee, with layer upon layer they were the height of fashion despite their lack of style. They were actually quite racy and were definitely a good-time skirt rather than one you wore to your great aunt's house for tea.

Headbands were fashionable in 1982 after Olivia Newton-John sported one for her video 'Physical' and actress Lisa Hartman wore one in an episode of *Knots Landing*. They remained in style until a year later. The craze started in California and was associated with other styles such as miniskirts and legwarmers.

Legwarmers were traditionally worn by dancers for dance practice and training. They were a functional garment that became overly popular when US TV series *Fame* hit front rooms on both sides of the Atlantic. Girls everywhere wore them literally everywhere.

BMX bikes

Cuts, grazes, broken bones and flesh wounds were all part and parcel of riding a

Above: Olivia Newton-John poses with her headband.

COLLEGE
LEARNING RESOURCE CENTRE

BMX bike in the early 1980s. This did, however, depend on how good you were, because the idea of the BMX biking was to emulate the motorcross heros of the day. Clever stunts and 'tricks' were the order of the day and it was a status symbol to have a number plate attached to the front of your bike.

Though BMX (bicycle motocross) had been around since the late 1960s when it became popular in California, it had taken a decade to reach the cultural mainstream. One of the prime movers was Bob Haro, who in 1978 launched the first freestyle BMX team and by 1981 was performing shows to enthusiastic crowds all over the Midwest, Eastern United States, and parts of Canada. He also appeared as a stunt rider in Steven

Spielberg's smash sci-fi movie ET which, released this year, did much to popularise the craze on a global basis.

Specially designed bicycles with 20-inch wheels flew out of the doors of cycle shops as the world's youth suddenly rediscovered pedal power.

ZX Spectrum

Home computing reached a new level on 23 April 1982 when Sir Clive Sinclair announced the launch of his ZX Spectrum. Competing against the BBC Micro Model A, Sinclair's machine boasted twice as many colours, had more usable RAM and a faster data transfer rate.

It was the computer that every boy yearned to have at home as it could play the latest arcade games such as Space Invaders and Pacman but also doubled up as a useful office tool with word

1980 1981 **1982** 1983 1984 1985 1986 1987 1988 1989

Above: Sinclair ZX Spectrum.
Below right: Sir Clive Sinclair.
Below left: A BMX rider performing a stunt.

REMEMBER THE EIGHTIES

processing, database and spreadsheet software. The main problem was that the most common way of loading the games was via a traditional cassette player and the games software would quite often fail to load.

Sinclair was forced to sell his business to Sir Alan Sugar's Amstrad following the disastrous sales of his C5 electric tricycle in 1985 that left him with reported losses of £7 million after fewer than 17,000 were sold.

MUSIC

March

Actor turned singer John Belushi, alias Jake Blues, breathed his last this month, aged just 33. The corpulent Chicago-born Belushi had first charted Stateside in 1978 with a version of the garage-band classic 'Louie Louie' from the film *National Lampoon's Animal House*. In this he played the crass Bluto Blutarski, a performance that not only typecast him as a 'beer-swilling fraternity goof' but also won him the leading role of Jake in 1980's *Blues Brothers* film alongside Dan Aykroyd (Elwood), the Canadian actor he'd starred alongside in US TV's Emmy Award-winning *Saturday Night Live*.

He was working on a movie script when he was found in a room at Los Angeles' Chateau Marmont hotel. The cause of death was an accidental overdose of cocaine and heroin that caused respiratory failure. James Taylor sang at his interment, while a leather-clad Aykroyd led the funeral procession to the cemetery on his motorcycle.

Having resuscitated his flagging post-Black Sabbath career with the help of manager Sharon Arden, Ozzy Osbourne was battling his demons afresh in March

Above: 'Saturday Night Live', the show that provided a launchpad for Chevy Chase, Eddie Murphy, Gilda Radnor, Bill Murray, Dan Aykroyd and John Belushi.
Below: John Belushi shortly before his death.

appeared to squirt three gallons of water over the inferno. We didn't receive any further help.'

In the aftermath of the accident, Ozzy's life once again began to spiral out of control. But his wife-to-be had the answer. 'Sharon said, "If Randy was alive, he'd want you to carry on". So I decided the best thing to do was to get back out on the road. It wasn't the most amazing show, but we did it.'

The rest is history. Osbourne would enter the twenty-first century as a reality TV star, headliner of the annual Ozzfest and occasional frontman of a re-formed Black Sabbath.

1982 after the tragic death while on a tour of the United States of guitarist and friend Randy Rhoads. Rhoads, 25, had hired a light plane in Leesburg, Florida, with the band's wardrobe mistress and driver to buzz their tour bus but, as Ozzy stated in a sworn affidavit to US authorities following the accident, all did not go according to plan.

'I was awoken from my sleep by a loud explosion. I immediately thought we'd hit a vehicle but, after getting out of the bus, I saw that a plane had crashed. I didn't know who was on the plane at the time. When we realised that our people were on the plane, I found it very difficult to get assistance from anyone…one small fire engine arrived which

1980 1981 **1982** 1983 1984 1985 1986 1987 1988 1989

Below: Ozzy Osbourne.

REMEMBER THE EIGHTIES

1980 1981 1982 1983 1984 1985 1986 1987 1988 1989

May

On the eve of a UK tour to promote the album 'Combat Rock', Clash frontman Joe Strummer and manager Bernie Rhodes hatched a plan to boost lacklustre ticket sales by having Strummer apparently go missing. The rest of the band were not informed of the scheme. Rhodes suggested that the singer should fly to Texas but instead he headed for Paris without telling Rhodes, pulling off the disappearing trick for real. The manager issued a press statement which concluded that Joe had 'probably gone away for a re-think.'

Strummer later gave his own version of what happened. 'It was something that I wanted to prove to myself, that I was alive. It's very much like being a robot being in a group. You keep coming along and keep delivering and keep being an entertainer and keep showing up and keep the whole thing going. Rather than go barmy and go mad, I think it's better to do what I did, even for a month. I just got up and went to Paris …without even thinking about it. I only intended to say for a few days but the more days I stayed the harder it was to come back because of the more aggro I was causing that I'd have to face there.'

The British dates were cancelled and frantic efforts made to locate the errant singer before the Clash's imminent American tour, the penalties for cancellation of which would have crippled them financially. Strummer was tracked down in Paris, where he had achieved anonymity by growing a beard, allowing him to run in the city's marathon without being recognised. He returned to his colleagues, with surprisingly little aggro, in time to appear at a festival in Holland. This was drummer Topper Headon's last gig with the Clash, signifying the end of the classic line-up.

July

The gold lamé sheen of ABC's 'Lexicon of Love' together with an ironic take on love songs combined to form an irresistible package, sending the album straight to the top of the chart on its release in July 1982.

The Sheffield outfit had started life as Vice Versa before fanzine writer Martin Fry joined and effectively seized control of the band's destiny. ABC were by no means an overnight sensation, having been tipped for stardom by the *New Musical Express* back in December 1980.

'Lexicon' was Trevor Horn's first major work as a producer and featured orchestration by future Art of Noise colleague Anne Dudley. Horn had previously

Below: The Clash.

44

the high point in the turbulent career of Dexy's Midnight Runners.

The band broke through in 1980 with their first chart topper 'Geno'. Leader Kevin Rowland cut a controversial figure, refusing to talk to the music press instead taking out adverts which contained essays putting his point of view. They 'kidnapped' the master tapes of their first album to renegotiate their record deal. This soured relations with the EMI label and led to a parting of the ways. Dexy's' line-up splintered soon afterwards.

Rowland put together a new band, swapping donkey jackets for dungarees to create an 'Irish gipsy' look. The fiddle and violin of the Emerald Express, jointly credited with Dexy's on the single, replaced the brass section. 'Come On Eileen' spent four weeks at Number 1 in August on its way to becoming the year's only million-selling single.

1980 1981 **1982** 1983 1984 1985 1986 1987 1988 1989

fronted the Buggles and was fresh from stints as singer with prog rockers Yes and producer of pop duo Dollar. He would go on to become a much sought-after studio boffin whilst ABC would struggle to repeat the success of their debut.

August

A worldwide Number 1, perennial party favourite 'Come On Eileen' was

Above: Martin Fry of ABC.
Below: Kevin Rowland lead singer of Dexy's Midnight Runners.
Below left: Trevor Horn, performer and record producer.

SPORT

Test and County Cricket Board bans 15 players

The disquiet that had been rumbling around in the game of cricket finally came to a head in March when the Test and Country Cricket Board banned 15 players for three years after their involvement with the 'rebel' tour to South Africa. The players involved included England stalwarts, Graham Gooch, Geoff Boycott, John Emburey and Derek Underwood.

Boycott, who had become the most prolific run scorer in Test history the previous December when battling against India in Delhi, had been one of the main organisers of the controversial tour. The team had taken to the field under the guise of an invitation XI, the members of which were clearly looking at the project as a money-making exercise, rather than the larger political picture, for at the time South Africa was regarded as a pariah on the international sporting stage. Every effort was being made to encourage SA to emerge from the dark ages and embrace multiracial sport: the tour did nothing to encourage this policy.

The other consideration had to be the upcoming English tours by Pakistan and India, whose governing bodies were obviously hostile to the South African junket. The TCCB's decision clearly found favour with both countries, as the two Test series took place as scheduled.

Many thought the absence of the 'rebels' from the English team may have weakened the

side throughout a demanding summer. But thanks to magnificent efforts from the likes of Botham and Randall, the missing faces did not become an issue and both Test series became triumphs for the home team under the leadership of Mike Brearley who retired in the September.

Eventually Graham Gooch would re-emerge as a major force in Test cricket but Boycott was viewed with a certain amount of suspicion thereafter.

Above: John Emburey and Derek Underwood.
Below: Geoff Boycott during the innings in which he became the highest run scorer in England Test history.

REMEMBER THE EIGHTIES

Football World Cup won by Italy

The World Cup eventually went to the talented Italy team, as they beat West Germany 3-1, the goals coming via the tournaments top scorer Paolo Rossi, Altobelli and Tardelli, with the single reply scored by Paul Breitner. The margin would have been even larger if the Italians had not missed a penalty.

The final in Madrid was described as an ill-tempered affair but the best team in the competition deservedly took the prize.

The opening game had produced an immediate shock when the holders Argentina suffered an unlikely defeat at the hands of Belgium but England's challenge had started with great optimism. The first round of group games, comprising a 3-1 win over France in Bilbao, a 2-0 beating of Czechoslovakia and a narrow 1-0 defeat of Kuwait. Topping the group took the team

into a second league format against West Germany and Spain, but two goalless draws consigned them to a journey home and further disappointment.

Scotland failed to advance beyond the early stages, the 5-2 win over New Zealand hardly preparing them for a one-sided clash with Brazil which was lost 4-1. They were destined to finish third in their group after a 2-2 draw against USSR.

Surprisingly, Northern Ireland topped their group with an encouraging set of performances, a wonderful 1-0 win over the host country Spain following draws against Yugoslavia and Honduras. They were finally undone in the second round, a 2-2 draw with Austria being wiped out by a 4-1 defeat at the hands of France.

In the semi-finals Rossi was in fine form scoring both goals as Italy overcame Poland to take them into the final. The other game went to a penalty shoot-out

1980 1981 **1982** 1983 1984 1985 1986 1987 1988 1989

47

Below: Marco Tardelli celebrates scoring for Italy in the final of the World Cup.

1980 1981 **1982** 1983 1984 1985 1986 1987 1988 1989

after France and West Germany had played out a 3-3 draw. The Germans, as is their wont, went through 5-4.

Kangaroos unbeaten

Australian Rugby League touring sides are normally a formidable proposition at any time but the 1982 version has correctly been hailed as the greatest side of all time. They became known as 'The Invincibles' after winning every game during their British tour and continuing the march into France.

The three tests against Great Britain for the Ashes produced scores of 40-4, 27-6 and 32-8, with the home side looking very much second best. In total 22 games were won, many at a canter. The total try count in GB and France numbered 166 for, 9 against.

The side was packed with outstanding incredibly athletic players, including Peter Sterling and the

relatively green Mal Meninga. The great Wally Lewis found it difficult to get off the bench, as the team took Rugby League into a new dimension and set new levels of excellence. Britain's Alex Murphy summed it up when he described them as a 'team of supermen'.

POLITICS & CURRENT AFFAIRS

Falkland Islands invaded by Argentina

At the beginning of April, Argentina carried out a long-standing threat to invade the Falkland Islands, a territory that had been a matter of dispute between Britain and Argentina for some considerable time.

Above: Italy are crowned World Champions.

REMEMBER THE EIGHTIES

Only a company of Royal Marines had been stationed on the islands at the time and despite a valiant attempt to repel the invaders, they had to surrender after the governor, Rex Hunt, could see that their position was hopeless as they fought in and around the environs of Government House. Luckily, no casualties were inflicted upon the marines.

The response from Her Majesty's Government was immediate and John Nott, the defence secretary announced that when ready, a substantial task force including two aircraft carriers, would be speeding its way to the Falklands, the distance of some 8,000 miles being only a minor problem.

In Argentina, General Galtieri, the leader of the ruling junta, could be seen waving to delirious crowds who had been looking for something positive to emerge from a troubled regime. In fact, it was always believed that the invasion took place in order to give the General time to cover up many of the problems in Argentinean society.

HMG was not swayed by the General's remarks when he claimed a wish to remain on good terms with

Below: British troops arriving in the Falklands.

1980 1981 **1982** 1983 1984 1985 1986 1987 1988 1989

military. The first, a car bomb, went off in Hyde Park just as a line of Blues and Royals horsemen were riding by, causing the deaths of two guardsmen, seven horses and injuring 17 members of the public. This action was believed to be one of the most callous acts of the IRA's bombing campaign.

The second, which exploded two hours later, went off under the bandstand in Regent's Park, killing six soldiers outright and inflicting injuries on 24 others, half of whom were reported as being in a critical state.

In typically British fashion, attention was drawn to a horse called Sefton who had survived the Hyde Park blast and underwent an extensive operation to remove shrapnel from his body. The 'will he live or won't he' scenario caught the public's imagination and

Britain and suggesting the Falkland islanders had nothing to fear from their new masters. This only made Maggie Thatcher and Co more determined to restore the status quo.

By June, the Argentinean commander Major-General Menendez found himself having to accept a ceasefire as his forces were coming under remorseless pressure from British troops and the conflict could have only one result. The ill-advised invasion had cost the lives of close to 1,000 troops, the vast majority of which were Argentinean.

Bombs in the royal parks

Carnage came to two of London's royal parks in July, when successive IRA bombs took their toll of the

Above: Margaret Thatcher leaving Downing Street on hearing the announcement that British Forces had landed in the Falkland Islands.

REMEMBER THE EIGHTIES

his survival somehow typified the public's resilience in the face of IRA action.

The death of Leonid Brezhnev

The state funeral of Leonid Brezhnev took place in Red Square in November and over 70 countries sent dignitaries to pay their respects on this sombre occasion. Brezhnev had been Soviet leader for eighteen years, a period only exceeded by Joseph Stalin and although many Stalinist ways had been dropped by the Communist Party before he came to power Brezhnev always carried the stance of the true hard-line believer.

His rise to the top had much to do with his association with Nikita Krushchev whom he had met in 1931 when becoming a member of the party proper. Prior to World War II he toed the party line and was rewarded with a political role which found him leaving the army in 1946 carrying the rank of major-general.

When Krushchev took power in 1953, upon Stalin's death, Brezhnev could be found right at his side and took a position which guaranteed his virtually running the country alongside the seemingly more powerful individual.

Although loyal to Krushchev, Brezhnev somehow got involved in the 1964 plot to oust the Soviet Union's nominal leader and, after the deed had been done, found himself in the driving seat. His eighteen years in power left a strange legacy, whereby the country consolidated itself as a super power but failed in its quest to solve internal monetary problems, much of which revolved around a failing agricultural policy. His venture into Afghanistan, which claimed many Soviet casualties, did not exactly go down well with a doubting public. Although pictures exist of him smiling broadly, his image was that of a dour, uncompromising man.

Leaders from around the world could hardly have guessed that, within a couple of years of Brezhnev's death, they would be dealing with a totally different type of Soviet leader in the shape of Mikhail Gorbachev.

1980 1981 **1982** 1983 1984 1985 1986 1987 1988 1989

Below left and right: Brezhnev applauds during a congress meeting and waves to crowds in Moscow's Red Square.

51

1983

FASHION, CULTURE & ENTERTAINMENT

Breakfast TV

TV-am was the Independent breakfast television service from 1 February 1983 until 1992 which broadcast from 6.00 a.m. to 9.25 a.m. on weekday mornings. It made television history by being the first national operator of an ITV franchise at breakfast time. It was meant to be the first breakfast time service in the UK, but the BBC beat ITV by a couple of weeks, launching *Breakfast Time* on BBC 1 on Monday 17 January. Hosted by Frank Bough and Selina Scott, it offered a mix of news, features and sport.

Michael Parkinson, David Frost, Angela Rippon, Robert Kee and Anna Ford were all lined up as presenters for TV-am, but each one of them also had a stake in the business. The headquarters of the show were at Breakfast Television Centre based in Camden, where a former Henleys garage was converted by Terry Farrell and still has the huge plastic egg cups on its roof. Weekday mornings were filled with *Daybreak* and *Good*

Morning Britain. Early ratings were disappointing and presenters Angela Rippon and Anna Ford were sacked while chief executive Peter Jay quit the show. Anne Diamond and Nick Owen took up the helm in late 1983 and producer Greg Dyke slowly managed to improve ratings.

After several years of unscheduled programming when technical staff went on

Above: Angela Rippon.
Below: Selina Scott.

52

strike, chief executive Bruce Gyngell sacked the striking technicians, order was restored and ratings began to improve. In terms of turnover, TV-am was the most profitable TV station in the world during the mid-1990s.

Over on BBC 1, Frank Bough and Selina Scott were supported by Kirsty Wark, John Stapleton and Sally Magnusson. Today, the show is presented by Dermot Murnaghan and Sian Williams (who was confirmed as the main replacement for Natasha Kaplinsky in 2006) who present each Monday to Thursday. They are complemented by Bill Turnbull and Susanna Reid who present the show from Friday to Sunday.

CD players

The arrival of the compact disc in 1983 signalled the end of the road for traditional records, although dedicated vinyl junkies still argue today that if you spend enough money on a turntable the sound is better than the digital format.

Originating from an idea by Dutch physicist Klass Compaan, the concept was further developed by Philips which resulted in a prototype disc a year later and a proposal in 1978 for a worldwide standard to be set. With Sony now in partnership, their proposal was accepted by the Digital Audio Disc Committee and major manufacturers two years later.

Made from pure polycarbonate plastic, the 12cm diameter discs are then coated with a thin layer of aluminium and lacquer. The player consists of three major components: the drive motor to spin the disc, the laser to read the information stored on the disc and the tracking device to enable the laser to follow the spiral track.

Billy Joel's '52nd Street' was the first album ever to be released on CD when it hit the shops in Japan in

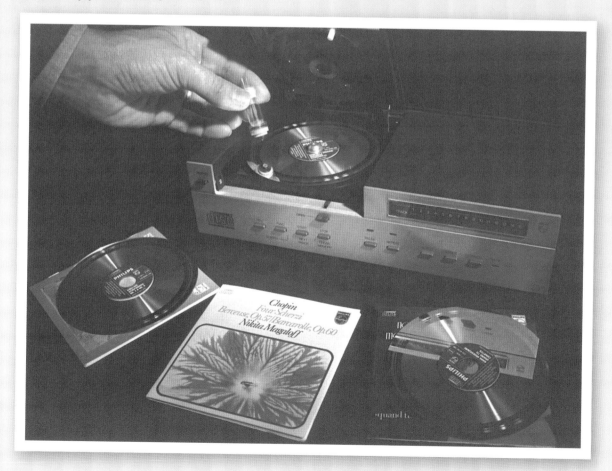

Below: A Philips technician gives a demonstration on how to use the new compact disc.

1980 1981 1982 **1983** 1984 1985 1986 1987 1988 1989

1982. Everyone else had to wait until the following year to experience the new audio format and even then the prices of both the CDs and the machines to play them on were expensive.

Dire Straits' 1985 album 'Brothers In Arms' was the first by a major rock act to fully utilise the facilities that CDs offered being digitally recorded and with longer and extra tracks than could be heard on vinyl or cassette. This attracted more customers and the price of discs and players began to reduce.

Further developments have been rapid with portable and in-car CD players arriving in 1984. Computers received CD-ROM drives the following year, and recordable CDs were first marketed in the late 1980s –

which have brought their own pirating problems – eventually leading to DVDs in 1996.

First laptop computer launched in US

May 1983 saw the marketing of the first true laptop computer when Gavilan Computer Corporation introduced the Gavilan SC. While other 'luggable' computers had been available for a couple of years – most notably the Osbourne 1 – they were about the weight of a portable sewing machine and had to be plugged into the mains in order to use them.

The Gavilan SC was the brainchild of company founder Manny Fernandez and weighed just 4 kilos. It featured a clamshell design where the screen folded down on top of the keyboard, a floppy disk drive and an internal modem, and would run on batteries, with a battery life of around nine hours according to the manufacturers.

Competing against the likes of the Sharp PC-5000 and the Compaq Portable, Gavilan ran into technological and cashflow problems when updating the machine and ceased business in 1985.

Power dressing/shoulder pads

With the popularity of American soaps such as *Dynasty* and *Dallas*, offices around the country became centres of power dressing. But it wasn't just the worker who adopted this fashion trend, women would wear jackets and complete suits to social functions as well.

Above: Billy Joel with his wife Christie Brinkley. His album '52nd Street' was the first ever released on CD.
Below: The Gavilan SC portable computer.

Dynasty costume designer Nolan Miller decided to emphasise Linda Evans' naturally broad shoulders and as a result every other actor found themselves with shoulder pads to keep things equal, and the fashion made the transition from screen to high street.

As shoulders got larger, so sleeves could be cut wider but the feminine look was kept by rolling the jacket sleeves up to reveal contrasting linings. Designers soon had enough of shoulder pads but public pressure demanded that they stay. In the end, they would be around till the early 1990s when women started cutting them out of the clothes they had just bought to create their own look.

David Niven dies

The magnificent actor David Niven died at the age of 73 from motor neurone disease in July 1983 and the tribute which appeared in his *Times* obituary – '…an archetypal English gentleman, witty, debonair, immaculate in dress and behaviour, but with mischief lurking never far from the surface' – sums him up perfectly.

James David Graham Niven was born in London on 1 March 1910 and decided to be an actor after resigning his commission in the Highland Light Infantry. He appeared in such 1930s successes as *The Charge*

1980 1981 1982 **1983** 1984 1985 1986 1987 1988 1989

Above: The cast of 'Dynasty' dressed in evening wear.
Below: David Niven.

Of The Light Brigade with Errol Flynn (1936) and *The Prisoner Of Zenda* (1937).

Niven is probably best remembered for his roles as nineteenth century explorer Phileas Fogg in *Around The World In 80 Days* and as the thief confounding Peter Sellers' Inspector Clouseau in *The Pink Panther* series of films. His autobiography *The Moon's A Balloon* has sold an amazing five million copies since it was first published in 1971.

MUSIC

February

Behind the wholesome façade of easy-listening duo the Carpenters lurked darkness. Richard Carpenter became

addicted to Quaaludes in the late-1970s whilst Karen developed anorexia nervosa, a psychological disorder associated with slimming, which would claim her life on 4 February 1983.

The siblings from southern California enjoyed massive popularity in the 1970s and the enormous workload which accompanied success undoubtedly contributed to the problems which derailed them at the end of the decade.

Karen's obsession with her weight reportedly began when an article in *Billboard* magazine described her as 'Richard's chubby sister'. Her battle with anorexia was largely unknown to the public until her death at 33 when the syndrome became the focus of widespread media attention. Immediately before she died, Karen

Below: Richard and Karen Carpenter.

worldwide. Released in December 1982, 'Thriller' had only reached Number 15 in the UK until 'Billie Jean', the second single from the album, took off. Four further tracks would be lifted from 'Thriller' for single release.

The video for the album's title track was a lavish horror spoof directed by John Landis of *Blues Brothers* and *An American Werewolf In London* fame. Released commercially as *The Making of Michael Jackson's Thriller*, the full-length version was a record-breaker in itself, shifting 100,000 copies in its first three days of release. Jackson's staggering level of fame, oddly childlike world view and increasingly bizarre behaviour would make him a fixture in the British tabloid press and later lead to his downfall.

New Order's 'Blue Monday', released in March 1983, became the biggest-selling 12-inch single ever but Factory Records lost 5p on every copy sold because of the cost of its elaborate sleeve. The record spent a total of 73 weeks in the UK chart between 1983 and 1985. The label was not expecting that level of success.

1980 1981 1982 **1983** 1984 1985 1986 1987 1988 1989

seemed on the verge of recovery, having gained 10lb in a week, but her body, weakened from years of dieting, could not cope and she suffered a fatal heart attack.

March

Michael Jackson dominated the British and American charts in this month with 'Billie Jean' and the LP 'Thriller' which would become the biggest-selling album of all time, with fifty million sales

Above: Michael Jackson performs on stage.
Below: New Order in concert.

1980 1981 1982 **1983** 1984 1985 1986 1987 1988 1989

New Order were formed in 1981 from the ashes of Joy Division, following the suicide of singer Ian Curtis. 'Blue Monday' grew out of their aversion to encores. The band were experimenting with primitive Apple Mac computers and synthesisers; this led to the idea of a song which could be played by machines when they had left the stage.

The 12-inch single was an innovation which emerged from the disco scene of the late-1970s as demand grew for longer mixes and better sound quality, 'Blue Monday' was only available in this format.

April

After a three-year hiatus punctuated only by some one-off singles and forays into acting, David Bowie returned

with a new album and single both entitled 'Let's Dance'. The interim period had seen the expiration of Bowie's deal with RCA Records. He signed a new contract with EMI America who triumphed in a bidding war to secure

his services. The deal was reported to be worth between $10 and $20 million.

'Let's Dance' was produced by Nile Rodgers, co-creator of Chic's international disco hits. Bowie and Rodgers assembled a new set of musicians to work on it, leaving no place for long-time rhythm guitarist Carlos Alomar whose duties were performed by Rodgers. Lead guitar was provided by Stevie Ray Vaughan. Out of nine songs, only five were brand new Bowie originals.

The album was Bowie's biggest commercial success so far, a transatlantic chart-topper. He reflected that the album and the accompanying Serious Moonlight

Above and below: David Bowie during a press conference and in concert.

Three years on, Bowie started to distance himself from the album. "Let's Dance", I think really, was more Nile's album than mine,' he said. 'It was Nile's vision of what my music should sound like, and I provided the songs.'

Bowie's star was to fall during the 1980s with the poorly received 'Tonight' and 'Never Let Me Down'. Although widely ridiculed, 1989's heavy rock 'Tin Machine' marked the beginning of an artistic recovery.

November

Not since the mid-1960s heyday of the Beatles-led British invasion of the American charts had UK acts enjoyed such success Stateside. In the vanguard were The Human League; 'Don't You Want Me' was a USA Number 1 in 1982. Dexy's Midnight Runners' 'Come One Eileen' topped the US charts in April 1983 and by November, almost a third of the *Billboard* listing was of British origin. The 1983 invasion was spearheaded by Duran Duran (three Top 10 hits in 1983) and Culture Club (four singles in the US top ten). Spandau Ballet and Wham! also made significant inroads in the States but the phenomenon was not limited to any single genre, or limited to old or new artists.

tour 'was significant in bringing me, as an entertainer, to a much larger audience than I had ever presumed would be interested.' Although warmly received by the critics, 'Let's Dance' surprised many fans who felt that Bowie was playing it safe and that the album lacked the depth of its predecessors.

With renewed interest in Bowie, RCA cashed in by releasing his back catalogue at mid price. By July, he had an unprecedented ten albums in the UK Top 100.

1980 1981 1982 **1983** 1984 1985 1986 1987 1988 1989

Above: Culture Club lead singer Boy George.
Below: George Michael and Andrew Ridgeley of Wham!

REMEMBER THE EIGHTIES

In the veteran category were the Animals, David Bowie, Elton John, the Kinks, the Moody Blues, Robert Plant and Rod Stewart. Cliff Richard's most successful period in the US had come three years earlier. His single 'Never Say Die (Give A Little Bit More)' could only reach Number 73. Newer faces like the Police,

the Eurythmics and Madness were represented along with Paul Young, Bonnie Tyler, Sheena Easton, Def Leppard, Asia and Elvis Costello. The ubiquitous Phil Collins was present both as a solo artist and with Genesis. Less celebrated bands such as the Fixx, Roman

Above: Rod Stewart.
Below: The Police.

American audiences were more conservative than their fickle British counterparts who quickly devoured each new movement before moving on to the next. Trends such as punk and 2 Tone made little impact on middle America, although their influence would eventually register in the 1990s.

Holiday, Naked Eyes and JoBoxers were also enjoying a taste of American success.

This represented a considerable upturn in the fortunes of British music in the USA where the charts seemed to be still suffering from the hangover of the late-1970s disco era.

1980 1981 1982 **1983** 1984 1985 1986 1987 1988 1989

61

Above left: Elvis Costello.
Above right: Sheena Easton.
Below left: Annie Lennox of the Eurythmics.
Below: Def Leppard.

REMEMBER THE EIGHTIES

SPORT

Tom Watson's fifth win at the British Open

In July, Tom Watson won his fifth British Open Golf Championship, his last win in a major event. The one-shot victory from Hale Irwin followed on from the previous year when he had secured both the British and US Opens, making him only the fifth man in history to achieve the double in the same year.

Born in Kansas City, Missouri in 1949, Watson had come to the sport relatively late in life while studying psychology at Stanford University, his natural aptitude allowing him to turn professional in 1971 after graduation. Three years later he won his first title at the Western Open, a prelude to his first British Open success in 1975 which heralded his arrival on the world stage.

In the space of nine years, Watson became the man to beat as he took eight major championships, two US Masters, One US Open and five British Opens.

He became the world's leading player, taking up the mantle of Jack Nicklaus whom he had beaten by one shot in an epic dual at the 1977 British Open.

In total, apart from those wins, Watson won 39 tournaments on the US PGA tour and on five occasions was leading money winner. He became a member of World Golf's Hall of Fame and in 1999 the Royal & Ancient Golf Club at St Andrews made him a life member. Only four other Americans had been graced with this latter honour. In 1991 he had effectively retired, only to start winning tournaments on the US Seniors Tour. There was no way that anyone would forget Tom Watson quickly.

When talking about the game's greatest players, invariably the names of Snead, Jones, Palmer, Player and Nicklaus are invoked.

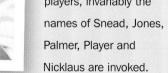

Below: Open Champion for 1983, Tom Watson.

REMEMBER THE EIGHTIES

Watson's performances from the mid-1970s to the early-1980s should qualify him for the list.

America's Cup win for Australia

The unthinkable finally happened in September when, after many years of trying, Australian business tycoon Alan Bond realised his dream and took the America's Cup away from the USA. This was the first time in 132 years of racing that this had happened.

For the 1983 series of seven races Bond had commissioned a yacht from designer Ben Lexcen which had a modified keel. Supposedly this would allow for greater manoeuvrability and would increase his chances of winning.

The series looked to be all over after *Liberty*, skippered by Dennis Conner, took a 3-1 series lead for the USA over the challenger *Australia II*. John Bertrand, the Australian skipper, adhered to his skills and managed to level at 3-3.

The stage was set for the best possible climax and despite Conner looking the likely victor as the final race progressed, Bertrand took advantage of a favourable wind to sail home by 43 seconds. The time and money Bond had ploughed into the project had paid off.

1980 1981 1982 **1983** 1984 1985 1986 1987 1988 1989

Below: Action from the America's Cup, 1983.

1980 1981 1982 **1983** 1984 1985 1986 1987 1988 1989

Sunil Gavaskar's 30th Test century

Madras, India was the place to be in December when Sunil Gavaskar took away Don Bradman's 35-year-old Test century record. Gavaskar scored 236 not out against the West Indies, in the process accumulating his 30th Test century which took him one beyond the great Australian. The story goes that, at the end of his innings, the West Indies wicket-keeper Dujon asked for and was given his bat as a souvenir. Gavaskar's prize from the Indian authorities was a car.

Gavaskar, a veritable run-making machine, had always looked capable of taking the record and would eventually amass a total of 34 centuries, which was only surpassed by his fellow countryman, the equally gifted Sachin Tendulkar in 2005. Gavaskar was always a joy to watch at the crease, with a correct technique, bags of concentration and as with all great batsmen, picking the correct ball to hit or leave alone. There wasn't a stroke in the book that he couldn't play with perfection and he displayed comfort on either the front or back foot. In 125 Tests he scored over 10,000 runs, at an average of 51.12, his highest score coming in that record-breaking Madras game.

In all first-class games he scored over 25,000 runs. The one-day game was not really his forte, his ultimate, assured run-getting technique relied on patience and did not lend itself to the mayhem often to be found in the shorter game. Nonetheless, his average of over 35 whilst accumulating over 3,000 runs is perfectly respectable.

Early in his Test career, some may forget that he actually opened the bowling on occasions, offering right-arm medium pace which only ever realised him one wicket.

Below: Sunil Gavaskar in action for India.

After retirement, Gavaskar, who had already made waves as a businessman, took up well received employment in the media world.

POLITICS & CURRENT AFFAIRS

Re-election of Margaret Thatcher

Margaret Thatcher became the first prime minister in over 30 years to be re-elected after experiencing a full term in Downing Street. The huge Conservative victory only confirmed what all the polls were indicating.

Maggie might have fallen from grace a few years on, but in 1983 she was far and away the most dominant personality in British politics. Other political leaders found if difficult to match her force of character and commitment to a cause.

The June election results made sorry reading for her opponents, as the Tories romped home with an overall majority of 144 seats, the biggest since the Labour win in 1945. The Labour Party had lost the total confidence of the country and in the south of England their vote descended to pitiful levels.

Casualties of the election were Michael Foot, the Labour leader and his Liberal-Social Democratic Alliance counterpart Roy Jenkins who would soon be replaced.

Korean airliner shot down by Soviet fighter

In September, a major diplomatic row blew up when a Soviet jet fighter shot down a scheduled Korean Airlines Boeing 747 as it flew over Sakhalin Island off the coast of Siberia. The ramifications were highly serious and the claims, followed by counter-claims, rumbled on for days afterwards.

1980 1981 1982 **1983** 1984 1985 1986 1987 1988 1989

Above: Margaret Thatcher speaking her mind.

REMEMBER THE EIGHTIES

The original Soviet announcement declared the aircraft had been on a spying mission to check out military locations, had been showing no lights in poor visibility and had failed to respond to radio contact, giving them carte blanche to protect their own territory. In keeping with the times, this would have been one of the standard reactions to the presence of an alien aircraft. Shoot first and ask questions afterwards!

Nearly a week passed by before the Soviet authorities gave an explanation as to the aircraft's disappearance, early speculation being that it had been forced to land.

The story was maintained and confirmed by a tape provided by the US to the United Nations, where the fighter pilot could be clearly heard announcing his attack sequence, which had been sanctioned by the Soviet military. For a number of days the Soviets stuck to their claim of justifiable action, although it quickly became clear that their position was untenable.

Eventually, a Soviet statement was issued not so much admitting a terrible error had been made but the language used conveyed a guilty verdict. It expressed regret over the deaths of innocent people and shared the sorrow of bereaved relatives. In the 1980s this was an unusual act on behalf of the Soviet government but they counteracted the gesture by somehow blaming the US for the incident in a passage from the same statement.

The attack claimed the lives of 269 people, leaving thousands to grieve in South Korea.

US troops invade Grenada

In a move that once again indicated the belief that the US were intended to be 'policemen of the world', American troops invaded the island of Grenada in

Below: US soldiers next to two armoured vehicles as they patrol the island of Grenada.

October, to supposedly stabilise a somewhat confused state of affairs.

The US action took place after Maurice Bishop, the island's prime minister, had been put under house arrest, by his military commander General Hudson Austin. This dramatic action had taken place at a time when a number of Cuban troops were evident on the island and the US, more than twitchy about anything pertaining to the land of Castro, felt it should take a hand.

The first wave of troops was joined by hundreds of marines, adding to a confused situation involving the release of Bishop by his followers and his subsequent disappearance after re-arrest. Those in diplomatic circles viewing from afar were not best pleased by the unfolding picture.

The British prime minister, who backed President Reagan on most counts, made known her displeasure,

urging him to think again and the United Nations took a very serious view on the matter, declaring the action to be 'a flagrant violation of international law'.

Reagan, on the other hand, refused to be swayed by his global critics, as he announced various reasons for the invasion. From the US point of view his arguments were valid, including the fear that the building of a new airport might give the opportunity for use by military aircraft and also the duty he had to protect US citizens resident on the island.

The action continued, combining air strikes with action on the ground, and very quickly the superiority of the invasion force overwhelmed the much smaller Cuban contingent.

Outsiders regarded the entire affair as a piece of American paranoia which manifested itself any time a suggestion of 'Reds in our backyard' became an issue.

Above: A camp where about 630 Cuban soldiers are detained in Point Salinas, three days after US troops invaded Grenada.

1980 1981 1982 1983 **1984** 1985 1986 1987 1988 1989

1984

FASHION, CULTURE & ENTERTAINMENT

Starlight Express opens

The musical *Starlight Express* opened at London's Apollo Victoria Theatre on 27 March 1984 to rave reviews. Composer Andrew Lloyd Webber had wanted to make a musical about the Reverend W Awdry's series of books featuring Thomas the Tank Engine and friends but could not agree with the author on the degree of control he wanted.

Originally written in the late 1970s as a Cinderella-type story for Webber's children, *Starlight Express* was adapted for the theatre by Webber (music) and Richard Stilgoe (lyrics) with the entire cast performing on roller skates. It was directed by Trevor Nunn, choreographed by Arlene Phillips and designed by John Napier, with the theatre being revamped to incorporate the track extending into the audience.

The story takes place in a child's dream where trains converge on a model railway for a racing tournament. The main characters are Rusty (the Cinderella figure), Greaseball and Elektra (the ugly sisters) and the Starlight Express (fairy godmother).

Rusty, a steam engine, dreams of winning the race but is thwarted by the underhand methods of the diesel

Below: Andrew Lloyd Webber (centre) with Stephanie Lawrence (right) star of the musical 'Starlight Express', and director Trevor Nunn.

68

Greaseball. Elektra, meanwhile, tries to steal the heart of Rusty's true love, Pearl the observation car. With his confidence dented, an old steam engine named Poppa tells Rusty about the Starlight Express, a midnight train who helps engines in trouble. After Poppa injures himself, Rusty says his prayers and is told he doesn't need help, just self-confidence. Needless to say, Rusty wins the tournament and he and Pearl live happily ever after.

There have been various versions around the world since, with perhaps the most notable being staged at the purpose-built Starlighthalle in Bochum, Germany, that opened in May 1988 and entertained its 11,111,111[th] customer on 5 April 2006. *Starlight Express* was updated to include new songs in 1992 but theatre-goers preferred the original and its long run ended in January 2002.

Britain loses three legendary entertainers

The world of television and film was in mourning this year after losing three of its favourite sons.

On 29 May, Eric Morecambe – one half of the comedy duo Morecambe and Wise – suffered a heart attack after six curtain calls following the end of a charity performance at Tewkesbury Theatre. The 58-year-old, whose real name was Eric Bartholomew, and who had been making audiences laugh for more than 40 years, failed to regain consciousness and died in hospital. At its 1970s peak, *The Morecambe & Wise Show* boasted viewing figures in excess of 20 million.

Yorkshire-born James Mason died on 27 July at the age of 75 from a heart attack in his home at Lausanne, Switzerland. Mason, born 15 May 1909, enjoyed a long and varied film career lasting from the mid 1930s until

Above: Comedy double-act Eric Morecambe and Ernie Wise.

1980 1981 1982 1983 **1984** 1985 1986 1987 1988 1989

Where Eagles Dare, and was nominated for seven Oscars without success. He also narrated Jeff Wayne's epic musical version of *War Of The Worlds* (1978). Burton, who was buried in Switzerland wearing a red suit in homage to his Welsh roots, always refused to work on 1 March, St David's Day.

Slogan T-shirts

his death. He starred in such movies as the 1940s costume melodramas *The Man In Grey* and *The Wicked Lady* as well as adventurous epics like *20,000 Leagues Under The Sea* in which he starred as Jules Verne's Captain Nemo alongside Kirk Douglas and *Journey To The Centre Of The Earth*.

Just nine days later, the legendary Richard Burton passed away after suffering a stroke. Like Morecambe, he was just 58-years-old. Burton, born Richard Walter Jenkins, was the youngest of 13 children and endured poverty in his younger years in a Welsh mining village. He appeared in numerous films including *Cleopatra* (with Elizabeth Taylor, whom he married twice) and

T-shirts bearing various slogans became the rage again after designer Katherine Hamnett introduced political comments in the fashion arena when she wore one to a meeting with Margaret Thatcher in 1984 that stated '58% don't want Pershing'. It was the perfect way for the youth to express their discontent with issues of the day such as high unemployment and the nuclear arms race.

Although the punk era had seen its own fair share of slogan T-shirts, this concept was also adopted by the

Above: James Mason.
Middle: Elizabeth Taylor and Richard Burton in a scene from the film, 'Cleopatra'.
Below: Richard Burton.

pop world with some of the first bearing the legends 'Relax – don't do it' and 'Frankie says relax' from Liverpudlian group Frankie Goes To Hollywood's chart-topping 'Relax'. That

when it was adopted by Yuppies (Young Urban Professionals) in the City who brandished it about. Prior to this revolution, the best way to store somebody's contact details had been on a Rolodex or a diary so the Filofax – a leather-bound ring binder approximately A5 in

song was banned by the BBC for its sexual connotations which made it go on to become an even bigger hit than it probably would have done.

Filofax

While the Filofax had been invented as long ago as 1921 by Norman & Hill Ltd in London, the design actually dated back to an American organising system from the First World War.

The Filofax (literally meaning file of facts) came to prominence around this time

size into which you could insert replacement address sheets and each year's diary – was perfect. You could even get computer software that would print out sheets at the correct size.

Nowadays, electronic organisers and personal data assistants have largely replaced the Filofax but there will always be some who prefer to keep their important details on something they can physically touch rather than trust it to a computer memory.

1980 1981 1982 1983 **1984** 1985 1986 1987 1988 1989

Above: Frankie Goes To Hollywood, who topped the charts in 1984 with their single 'Relax'.
Below: Filofax range.

1989 1988 1987 1986 1985 **1984** 1983 1982 1981 1980

human revolt against the computers.

The movie, Cameron's first feature film, was shot for a measly $6.5 million but went on to earn more than $38 million in 1984 alone. It was memorable for its groundbreaking special effects and Schwarzenegger's catchphrase 'I'll be back'.

MUSIC

February

After 22 years of constant touring, Status Quo announced that their forthcoming UK dates would be their last. The End of

Terminator

One of the biggest and most surprising box office successes of 1984 was without doubt *Terminator*, directed by James Cameron and starring former bodybuilder Arnold Schwarzenegger and Linda Hamilton. It was the first in a trilogy with *Terminator 2: Judgement Day* being released in 1991 and *Terminator 3: The Rise Of The Machines* eight years later.

It told the story of a humanoid robot (Schwarzenegger) who has been sent back from the year 2029 where machines rule the Earth to 1984. Its mission is to kill Sarah Connor (Hamilton) before she can give birth to her son who will, in the future, lead the

Above: Arnold Schwarzenegger as the 'Terminator'.
Below: Status Quo in concert.

making a hasty decision and we all wanted to go out on a high.'

The move was prompted by musical differences with bassist Alan Lancaster. Quo were persuaded out of retirement to open Live Aid with 'Rocking Around The World' and subsequently began work on a new album. In the meantime, Lancaster had emigrated to Australia and unsuccessfully tried to prevent his former colleagues from using the name. Rossi and guitarist Rick Parfitt would continue as Status Quo for another 22 years and counting...

April

On 1 April, the day before his 45th birthday, soul singer Marvin Gaye was shot and killed by his father Marvin Gaye Senior. Although the two had apparently been arguing about 'an insurance matter', the background to the artist's death was more complex. Relatives claimed that Marvin had threatened to commit suicide several times after moving back into his parents' house and that during several bitter arguments with his father, Gaye pushed him to the limit. This, it was said, represented a deliberate ploy aimed at forcing his father to kill him as an alternative to suicide. Marvin Senior was sentenced to five years probation after pleading guilty to voluntary manslaughter.

Shortly before, the singer had endured health problems whilst touring to promote the album 'Sexual Healing', finding his newly-revived level of fame difficult to handle. Drug addiction and paranoia led to him being surrounded by bodyguards and, ironically, often wearing a bullet-proof vest.

the Road tour comprised 35 dates, including seven nights at London's Hammersmith Odeon.

Singer Francis Rossi explained their reasoning. 'We feel that everything has to come to an end sometime. And this seems to us like the right time. No one could accuse us of

1980 1981 1982 1983 **1984** 1985 1986 1987 1988 1989

Above: Soul singer Marvin Gaye.

Gaye (the 'e' was an affectation in honour of his hero Sam Cooke) was one of Tamla Motown's top male singers in the early 1960s. Like Stevie Wonder, he fought against the restrictions of the label's hit making process, particularly the practice of dividing performers, songwriters and producers into separate camps. In Britain, he was best known for the 1969 chart-topper 'I Heard It Through The Grapevine' which was a hit again in 1986 when used in a jeans commercial. He duetted with several female singers, most notably Tammi Terrell. After Terrell died of brain cancer in 1970, Gaye went

into seclusion, re-emerging with the classic 'What's Going On', an album which explored political issues, leaving Motown head Berry Gordy initially reluctant to release it. After that his music shifted focus again with 'Let's Get It On', described by one reviewer as 'unparallelled in its sheer sensuality and carnal energy.'

A groundbreaking approach to in-concert rock films was demonstrated by Talking Heads with *Stop Making Sense* which premiered in April 1984. Shooting took place over three nights the previous December at the Pantages Theatre, Hollywood whilst the band was

Below: Talking Heads.

touring to promote their 1983 album 'Speaking In Tongues', the Heads' commercial breakthrough in America. The movie was the first to be made entirely using digital audio techniques and was directed by Jonathon Demme who would go on to helm *Silence of the Lambs* and *Married to the Mob*.

Talking Heads were a product of the late-1970s New York New Wave scene, having played their first gig at the legendary venue CBGB supporting the Ramones in 1976. Led by Scottish-born David Byrne, the band released a series of critically acclaimed albums. Byrne's visual flair was evident in the band's promotional videos, notably for the single 'Once In A Lifetime'.

Stop Making Sense was unusual for a rock movie in several respects. Only during the final song is there a direct shot of the audience – prior to that the crowd can only be glimpsed during wide shots or those taken from the back of the stage. An embargo on coloured lights led to the creation of innovative lighting techniques. Byrne insisted that the stage was kept free of distractions such as water bottles and that props were painted matt black so as not to reflect light.

The movie was carefully choreographed to reveal the process of staging the gig. It begins with Byrne alone on a bare stage singing 'Psycho Killer' accompanied only by a boom box. The set is built around him as the other performers arrive on stage one by one. By the film's climax, Byrne's uptight persona has loosened up and morphed into the wearer of the famous 'big suit'.

November

1984 was the year of Frankie Goes To Hollywood, the band, fronted by the openly gay Holly Johnson, whose first two singles 'Relax' and 'Two Tribes' hit Number 1 in a blaze of publicity and, in the former's case, a Radio 1 ban thanks to offended DJ Mike Read.

November saw Frankie's Trevor Horn-produced first album, 'Welcome To The Pleasuredome', follow the singles to the summit with the biggest ever ship-out of an album in Britain – 1,099,500 copies, representing over £5 million worth of business. It would later be rumoured that the Liverpudlian five-piece had been aided in their studio endeavours by a number of Ian Dury's Blockheads, but equal credit must go to the ex-10cc duo of Kevin Godley and Lol Creme for their imaginative videos – the one for 'Two Tribes', with Cold War warriors Reagan and Brezhnev fighting it out in the boxing ring, remains a classic today.

1980 1981 1982 1983 **1984** 1985 1986 1987 1988 1989

Below: Frankie Goes To Hollywood.

REMEMBER THE EIGHTIES

After seven years of fruitless 'Purple To Reform' headlines, Messrs Gillan, Glover, Blackmore, Lord and Paice finally headed out on a world tour – their first to feature the 'classic' line-up for over a decade – with their triple-platinum reunion album 'Perfect Strangers' sitting pretty at Number 5 here and Number 17 in the States.

The tour, which kicked off in Australasia, had an early highlight when George Harrison (a neighbour of Jon Lord, and introduced by singer Ian Gillan as 'Arnold from Liverpool') unexpectedly got up in Adelaide to jam along to the rock'n'roll standard 'Lucille'. The jaunt proved successful, lucrative and nearly strife-free ('the peace and quiet of the first-class lounge makes the downside of rock'n'roll worthwhile', sighed a temporarily contented Gillan), but it wasn't to last. By the time of the 1987 follow-up, old personality conflicts were again

Below: Deep Purple in the 1970s.

dancing gold medal for Great Britain's Jayne Torvill and Christopher Dean.

The event had not long been admitted into the Olympics, being regarded more as an entertainment than sport.

The Russians had always been the front-runners but Britain had experienced moments of success at world level in the past.

coming to the fore and the antipathy between the singer and guitarist Ritchie Blackmore would lead to the former's departure from the ranks for a second time in mid 1988.

SPORT

Torvill and Dean's Olympic Gold

In February, what was to become the most famous ice-skating routine in history took the Sarajevo Winter Olympics by storm and secured the ice-

Although favourites to take a medal of some colour, nobody was quite prepared for the couple's 'Bolero' routine which, with its techniques and artistic perfection, completely overwhelmed both their rivals and judges. They were awarded nine straight maximum scores for artistic impression, amidst jubilant scenes at the rink and much rejoicing from Olympic TV watchers at home. Subsequently, ice dancers have aspired to match such perfection.

Above, middle and below: Jayne Torvill and Christopher Dean perform 'Bolero', receive maximum points on the scoreboard and pose with their gold medals.

1980 1981 1982 1983 **1984** 1985 1986 1987 1988 1989

REMEMBER THE EIGHTIES

Los Angeles Olympic Games

Before the LA Olympics had started, everybody knew that the Eastern bloc countries would boycott the event, in a tit for tat reaction to American's absence from Moscow four years earlier. For some reason Romania chose to follow their own path and participated anyway.

In 1936, Jesse Owens had won four gold medals in Berlin for the USA, taking the 100 metres, 200 metres, the long jump and as a member of the 2 x 100 metres relay squad. Carl Lewis was expected to equal this feat and duly obliged in spectacular fashion which singled him out as the star of the games.

His win in the 200 metres marked a new Olympic record and his anchor leg in the relay helped the USA to

a new world record. Other notable athletic victories for the home country came from Roger Kingdom in the 100 metres hurdles and Edwin Moses, the greatest ever performer at 400 metres hurdles.

Great Britain were not without success in the track and field, Sebastian Coe led home Steve Cram to retain his 1,500 metres title and also grabbed a silver in the 800 metres. Daley Thompson again took gold in the

Above: Steve Ovett, Steve Cram and Sebastian Coe in action in the 1500m final during the 1984 Los Angeles Olympic Games.
Below: Carl Lewis cruises to victory in the 100m final.

78

decathlon and Tessa Sanderson became the first Briton to win an Olympic throwing event title in the javelin. Mick McLeod won a worthy silver in the 10,000 metres, Charlie Spedding gained a bronze for the marathon and a welcome silver came via the 4 x 400 metres team.

shores of the UK at the end of the tour as the first international eleven to win a full Test series 5-0 away from home.

Only one match ended in defeat during the summer and that was a one-day international. 'The Windies' as

The games contained its normal amount of controversy on the track, as Finland's Martti Vainio was disqualified for drug-taking after finishing second in the 10,000 metres and the famous Mary Decker/Zola Budd tripping incident rumbled on.

Predictably the USA picked up a whole hatful of gold metals, with the pool and boxing arena particularly kind to them.

The 'Blackwash'

Even by West Indian cricketing standards the 1984 touring team were just a little bit special. They left the

Above: Tessa Sanderson throws the javelin during the 1984 Olympic Games.
Below: West Indies fast-bowler Malcolm Marshall in mid-air action.

REMEMBER THE EIGHTIES

1980 1981 1982 1983 **1984** 1985 1986 1987 1988 1989

they were known, spent the year demolishing the opposition and completed a record run of 11 straight Test victories which took over two decades to better.

This team bristled with talent, Viv Richards and Clive Lloyd spearheading the batting, backed up by one of the most fearsome fast bowling attacks the game of cricket has ever witnessed. These were the days of Garner, Holding and Marshall, all at their peak and able to give even the most assured of batsman a tough time of it. As a unit this side compare favourably with any past West Indian team.

The less experienced members of the England team were given a torrid time by the trio. Bruises and broken bones were the order of the day for those unprepared for the onslaught and even the older hands struggled to make an impression against the most hostile of bowling. To put the quality of the opposition in perspective the England team, captained by David Gower, included Ian Botham, Allan Lamb and Bob Willis. Although winning one of the limited over games, the home side were put to the sword at Old Trafford when Richards scored a one-day record 189 not out. The WI

Above: Viv Richards hooks Derek Pringle of England for another four on his way to a record 189 not out during the one day International played at Old Trafford.

Test series win became affectionately referred to as 'The Blackwash'.

To show that England were not the only side to suffer at the hands of the West Indian quickies, two amazing statistics were worth repeating. During the year, Garner took a total of 79 wickets and Marshall bagged 73.

POLITICS & CURRENT AFFAIRS

The Battle of Orgreave

The coal strike had lasted for some twelve weeks when the dispute witnessed its worst outbreak of violence at the end of May. Substantial numbers of pickets clashed with large numbers of police officers outside the Orgreave coking plant. Mounted police were called into action, chasing the strikers over a field, while their colleagues on foot resorted to riot gear as the confrontation became increasingly ugly.

Blame for the escalation in violence saw both sides pointing the finger at the other. Arthur Scargill, president of the National Union of Mineworkers, likened the actions of the constabulary to those employed in a police state such as Chile. In turn, the police regarded Scargill's presence as inflammatory and believed he should shoulder responsibility.

Part of the pickets' frustration came from their inability to stop lorries from passing in and out of the plant, plus they were angry over steel workers walking through the lines to carry on working rather than joining them in their cause.

The strike lasted a year before the dispute was eventually settled and became the last major face-off between the miners and government.

During the year, some miners had never stopped working, the Nottinghamshire

Above and below: Policemen outside a pit during the miners strike and surrounding striking coalminers.

1980 1981 1982 1983 **1984** 1985 1986 1987 1988 1989

1980 1981 1982 1983 1984 1985 1986 1987 1988 1989

Gas Leak at Bhopal kills over 2000

In December, the city of Bhopal in India became the scene of a major disaster, when a storage tank at a chemical factory leaked the noxious gas methyl isocyanate into the atmosphere, causing 2,000 deaths and affecting close to 200,000 others. The immediate symptoms shown by the suffering thousands included kidney and liver failure plus many cases of blindness.

The first statements from medical staff suggested knock-on effects in the future. Reports of dead bodies, both human and animal, lying in the streets were confirmed as troops arrived to bring some order to the scenes of carnage.

The finger of blame was pointed at the owners of the plant, American Union Carbide, when revelations appeared in a newspaper to the effect that leaks had occurred at the location in the past. The

pitmen being a case in point, and over its months numbers of union members took the bull by the horns and returned of their own volition.

The big losers at the end of the day were the NUM, whose funds were frozen in November after the High Court declared the strike to be illegal. A large fine was imposed on the union and on Scargill a much smaller personal fine. Much of the NUM's power dissipated after the event and its president's status within the trade union movement in general declined accordingly.

Above: The Bhopal factory after the gas leak.
Below: A victim of the Bhopal tragedy.

company made all the correct noises as to responding to compensation claims but years later the Bhopal incident was still subject to discussion in the courts as claims lingered on.

Assassination of Indira Gandhi

In June this year Indian troops had stormed the Golden Temple in Amritsar to remove hundreds of Sikh militants from the holy shrine. The operation had intended to be handled in such a way as to keep casualties to a minimum but had turned into a bloodbath, claiming the lives of over 900 souls, 700 of which were Sikhs.

The Indian prime minister, Indira Gandhi, had about her a number of Sikh bodyguards whom she trusted implicitly but even their commitment to Mrs Gandhi was stretched beyond breaking point after events at Amritsar.

As she wandered through her garden in New Delhi, her bodyguards took their retribution and shot her ten times. One of the Sikhs was killed instantly with the other being wounded. Reports said she had been going to meet Peter Ustinov, who was making a documentary about her, when the killers struck.

Mrs Gandhi had not always been the most popular of political figures and the instant successor, her son Rajiv would also receive a similarly rocky ride in the job. In the immediate future, he made a nationwide broadcast for calm as violence erupted all over India, Hindus and Sikhs were in a seriously distrustful mood and no quarter would be given as rampaging Hindus wrecked vengeance for the prime minister's death. Over 1,000 people lost their lives in the ensuing riots, acts of arson and butchery, which were only terminated by the intervention of troops.

The name Gandhi is synonymous with assassination and Rajiv became the third high profile politician with that name to be murdered in 1991.

1980 1981 1982 1983 **1984** 1985 1986 1987 1988 1989

Above: Rajiv Gandhi, his wife Sonia (2nd right) and their daughter Priyanka (3rd right) at the cremation of Indira Gandhi.

1985

FASHION, CULTURE & ENTERTAINMENT

Orson Welles dies

Notorious film director Orson Welles died of a heart attack on 10 October 1985 – the same day as actor Yul Brynner – while sitting at his typewriter at his Los Angeles Hollywood home.

Born George Orson Welles on 15 May 1915 in Kenosha, Wisconsin, his mother died when he was just nine and as a child prodigy he was enrolled at the Todd School two years later where he met Roger Hill, the headmaster who would be a father figure to him. It was here that Welles' interest in films surfaced and he began writing, directing and performing. His first film attempt was 1934's *The Hearts Of Age*, a four-minute silent movie.

The film many consider to be his greatest triumph was 1941's *Citizen Kane* that won an Oscar for Best Writing (Original

Above and below: Orson Welles shortly before he died and in his role as Charles Foster Kane in the film 'Citizen Kane', which he wrote, produced, directed and starred in.

1980 1981 1982 1983 1984 **1985** 1986 1987 1988 1989

Screenplay). It is acknowledged as a milestone in the development of cinematic technique.

As well as directing the movie, Welles starred in the title role of Charles Foster Kane, a man who cannot openly love but instead insists on relationships being on *his* terms. He goes through life without finding his true love and dies alone, a recluse in his big but dilapidated house. The film was rumoured to be based on newspaper mogul William Randolph Hearst, but some critics believe it to be a prediction of how Welles' own life would turn out: he was married three times, including to actress Rita Hayworth between 1943-45.

Described by some as one of the greatest directorial geniuses to have graced Hollywood along with Charlie Chaplin, Welles himself rated *The Trial* (1962) and *Chimes At Midnight* (1966) as greater achievements than *Citizen Kane*. He never really fulfilled his potential, however, as he had a habit of alienating the wrong people and as a result never received the financial backing his talents deserved.

EastEnders

First broadcast on 19 February 1985, *EastEnders* was never expected to last. Critics said it was too depressing and that the characters lacked the warmth and depth of rival soaps such as *Coronation Street*. However, it became hugely popular, has been running for more than 20 years and is often the UK's highest rated programme. It won seven British Soap Awards in May 2006 including the 'Best British Soap' award.

Set in the fictional London Borough of Walford, *EastEnders* is primarily based in characters' homes and the local pub, the Queen Victoria, in fictional Albert Square. Senior designer Keith Harris designed and built the set for *EastEnders* which over the years has seen the extension of the fourth side of Albert Square, Turpin Road, George Street and Walford East tube station.

The characters of *EastEnders* are often built around strong families such as the Fowlers, the Beales and the Mitchells. Co-creator, Tony Holland was from a large East End family and families within the show typify the East End spirit and gritty determination often under the watchful eye of a matriarch, such as Lou Beale.

Storylines have over the years been fascinating and based on real issues and while established older characters such as Dot Cotton play an essential part

Above: John Lydon with actress Linda Davidson, who played punk Mary in 'Eastenders'.

1980 1981 1982 1983 1984 **1985** 1986 1987 1988 1989

1985 1989 1988 1987 1986 1984 1983 1982 1981 1980

wanted the show to be realistic. This led to storylines such as cot death, homophobia, rape, teenage pregnancy, drugs, prostitution, mixed-race relationships, sexism, divorce, racism, muggings, HIV, alcoholism and domestic violence. The show even covered the issue of euthanasia and later followed it with a storyline about incest.

Coca-Cola announces new formula

Popular fizzy drink manufacturer Coca-Cola announced a new formula on 23 April 1985 simply labelled New Coke. Such was the public's reaction to the change, however, that the company re-introduced the old formula on 10 July and sales of the drink they relabelled Coke Classic rocketed.

Surveys had indicated that, while most rival Pepsi drinkers were loyal to their brand, Coke drinkers would quite happily drink something else. This prompted the company to launch the new formula in 1985, Coke's centennial year, with the slogan 'The best just got better'.

there is usually a businessman (often involved in crime) who is seen as both a threat and a local authority figure. Den Watts who first ran the Queen Vic, James Wilmott-Brown who raped Kathy Beale, Steve Owen who clashed with the Mitchell brothers on more than one occasion and Johnny Allen are all credited with being this character.

Programme makers wanted to ensure the show was about everyday life in an inner city and especially

Above: Anita Dobson who played Angie Watts in 'Eastenders' with Brian May from Queen.
Below: A can of New Coke.

REMEMBER THE EIGHTIES

The new formula was reintroduced as Coke II in 1990 but had disappeared by the end of the twentieth century.

Goths

Gothic music became extremely popular in post-punk 1985 with groups such as the Damned, the Cure, Sisters of Mercy and Siouxsie and the Banshees enjoying chart hits. Bauhaus, formed in Northampton in 1978, are widely regarded as being the first gothic band.

Fashions changed as well as musical taste, with teenagers wearing the black outfits, black eye make-up and lipstick set against pale foundation and dyed black hair to give a very dark image. By the mid 1990s, the genre had adopted Victorian styles and embraced some of the more morbid beliefs of that era. It is one of the most enduring musical and fashion trends with Goths still widespread today.

The original Goths were a German tribe who had contributed to the fall of the Roman Empire but that term later became used to describe barbarians and eventually took on horror connotations. *Dracula* is the most famous Gothic novel ever written.

Protesters campaigning against the change formed action groups and filed a civil lawsuit against the company whose roots dated back to 1884 when Georgian druggist John Stith Pemberton invented his French Wine Coca. With prohibition legislation, he developed a non-alcoholic version and called it Coca-Cola, originally sold as a patent medicine.

Above: The Damned.
Middle: The Cure.
Below: A Goth.

1980 1981 1982 1983 1984 **1985** 1986 1987 1988 1989

REMEMBER THE EIGHTIES

1980 1981 1982 1983 1984 **1985** 1986 1987 1988 1989

Al-Fayeds take over Harrods

On 11 March 1985 it was announced that the Al-Fayed brothers – Mohamed and Ali – had paid £615 million to gain control of the House of Fraser and in doing so became the new owners of London's prestigious Harrods store. The two brands were de-merged in 1994 with the Al-Fayeds keeping control of Harrods.

Harrods, launched in 1835 by Charles Henry Harrod and moved to its present location in 1849 when he became worried about a cholera epidemic sweeping the capital, has since become *the* cult shop in London with some people visiting the store to buy a small item just to be seen carrying a bag bearing the famous name.

Mohamed Al-Fayed became chairman of Fulham Football Club in 1997, the same year that his son Dodi perished in the controversial car crash in Paris that claimed the life of Diana, Princess of Wales.

MUSIC

June

Bruce Springsteen was 1985's biggest rock star. 'Born In The USA' went quadruple platinum in UK and sold 14 million copies across the globe. His world tour was seen by an estimated two million people and, in June, Springsteen arrived for the British leg comprising six

Below: Exterior of Harrods Department Store.

Ronald Reagan's 1984 re-election campaign, its double-edged message notwithstanding. 'Dancing in the Dark' gave Springsteen his UK first top ten single when reactivated in 1985. The video featured a young Courteney Cox, later of *Friends* fame.

Springsteen was without equal as a live performer, maintaining a sense of intimacy during stadium shows by talking to the audience. 'It just seemed like the normal thing to do. I always saw the audience as a person, no matter how big the crowd is,' he explained. 'The stories just came and they offset the songs a little bit.' I like to play the ones that are my favourites and favourites of the guys in the band and I try to put together a show that covers a lot of ground and people come and get their money's worth.'

Another feature of his gigs was their length, often in excess of four hours. 'I wrote a bunch of songs and I like to play the ones that people come to hear.'

Flamboyant shock-rockers Sigue Sigue Sputnik signed to EMI in June 1985 amidst a flurry of hype, most of it generated by the band itself who claimed that the deal was worth £4 million. The advance was later revealed to be less than £100,000. Statements like

enormous open-air shows, two in Newcastle, three at Wembley and one in Leeds. He was accompanied, as ever, by the E Street Band.

The previous twelve months had seen Springsteen rise from cult figure to international star, nicknamed 'the Boss'. 'Born In The USA' was the seventh album in a recording career which stretched back to 1973 and which had survived the hype proclaiming him 'the future of rock and roll' on his first visit to London in 1975.

The album's title track was controversially co-opted for President

Above: Bruce Springsteen on stage.
Below: Tony James from Sigue Sigue Sputnik with Bob Geldof and Janet Street-Porter.

'We are going to be the greatest rock 'n' roll band ever' made them notorious before they released a record.

Sputnik were put together by former Generation X bassist Tony James, whose aim was to create a band with an outrageous visual image. Consequently, he recruited people on the basis of how they looked, regardless of their musical ability. Their debut single, 'Love Missile F1-11', reached number three in May 1986 and the album 'Flaunt It' featured advertising in the space between tracks. Success, however, was fleeting and the backlash quickly began, summed up by a *New Musical Express* headline: 'Would you pay £4m for this crap?'

July

Dubbed 'the Global Jukebox' by Bob Geldof, the story of Live Aid began late in 1984 when the charity single 'Do They Know It's Christmas?' was recorded by Geldof and Midge Ure together with a host of pop stars under the name Band Aid. The record was inspired by Geldof watching Michael Buerk's BBC news report of the famine in Africa. At first, Geldof's ambitions were modest. 'It was just a personal gesture,' he said.

Above: Bono of U2 during their iconic performance at Live Aid.
Below: The huge crowd at Wembley gathered to witness one of the greatest concerts of all time.

REMEMBER THE EIGHTIES

'I thought 72,000 sales, give the money to Oxfam and Save the Children and get the fuck out.' Three million copies later, Bob came to realise that the cause resonated deeply with the public.

During a visit to Africa, Geldof recognised that,

massive dash to set up an organisation that would handle that influx of money and distribute it on a rational basis,' he recalled. 'That was frightening.'

Through a combination of serendipity and Geldof's stubborn refusal to take no for an answer from anyone, Live Aid went ahead on 13 July from Wembley Stadium and JFK Stadium, Philadelphia. The first choice American venue, New York's Shea Stadium, was unavailable.

despite USA for Africa's 'We Are the World' single, greater effort was needed and the idea of an all-star concert was conceived in March 1985, leaving just twenty weeks to organise not only the biggest gig the world had ever seen but also the machinery to dispense the proceeds. '1985 was a

Some of the biggest names of 1980s rock put their egos aside to perform fifteen-minute sets. At Wembley, Queen and U2 played two of the event's most talked about music whilst Madonna triumphed Stateside. Phil Collins' busy day consisted of solo sets on both sides of the Atlantic plus accompanying Sting in London and, in Philadelphia, drumming for Eric Clapton and for Led Zeppelin, the only public reunion of that band's surviving members.

Above: All the acts that performed at Wembley gather for the final song 'Do They Know It's Christmas'.

1980 1981 1982 1983 1984 **1985** 1986 1987 1988 1989

1980 1981 1982 1983 1984 **1985** 1986 1987 1988 1989

August

Madonna was crowned Queen of Pop in 1985, achieving two Top Ten albums and no less than seven Top Ten hits in Britain, a run of success which included first and second spots in the singles chart in mid-August with 'Into the Groove' at Number 1 and the re-released 'Holiday' nestling just behind. She also appeared in the title role of the movie *Desperately Seeking Susan* which was on general release in 1985.

Born Madonna Louise Veronica Ciccone in Bay City, Michigan and raised in Detroit, she is not only the most successful female singer of all time but also the most successful female producer and songwriter. Madonna has never been afraid to court controversy, notably over her *Sex* book and 'Erotica' video.

Affectionately known as 'Madge' in the UK, she now resides with film director husband Guy Ritchie in London, where she claims to enjoy the odd pint of real ale.

SPORT

Dennis Taylor wins World Snooker Championship

The April World Snooker Championships at the Crucible in Sheffield was graced by a final that nobody who witnessed it will ever forget. The game, which extended beyond midnight and kept millions of TV viewers glued to their seats, was exactly what the sport needed after a drugs scandal had blighted the British Open earlier in the year.

This brought together Steve Davis, the Champion from the previous two years, and the popular Irishman Dennis Taylor. Inevitably Davis started as a strong favourite and over the first 34 frames Taylor had never managed to get ahead, although he never quite lost touch.

In the final frame, Davis had only to pop an easy black to retain his title but inexplicably missed. In a moment of drama only high quality sport can engender, Taylor took his place at the table and clinched the most unlikely of results.

Above: Madonna in concert at Madison Square Garden.
Middle: Dennis Taylor becomes Snooker World Champion after defeating Steve Davis in a thrilling final.

Boris Becker wins Wimbledon

In July, the 17-year-old German Boris Becker became the youngest ever men's singles winner at Wimbledon, when he beat South African Kevin Curren.

The match had started well for Becker as he took the first set 6-3, Curren fought back to grab a tie-break second, the German reversing the situation in the third and finally running out 6-4 winner in the fourth.

His athleticism, enthusiasm and powerful serve and volley game added to the excitement for the spectators who witnessed this piece of Wimbledon history. This was a far cry from his exit the previous year by way of a wheelchair after suffering a bad injury during a third round match.

Becker had already signalled that he could be a contender for the title when he won the pre-Wimbledon tournament at Queen's Club, beating Cash, McNamee and Kriek in the process. In the earlier rounds at Wimbledon he had become involved in a couple of five-setters, which might have taken its toll of an older man but seemingly built up his belief that he could win the title.

During the rest of the year Becker won two further titles, Ivan Lendl the one obstacle in his way. Lendl beat him in Tokyo, New York and at Wembley.

In 1985, Becker won a total of seven titles, overcoming Lendl a couple of times, most satisfyingly in a straight sets win at Wimbledon as he retained the championship. Always a popular visitor to south-west London, in subsequent years he always appeared to be threatening to take the title again and in 1989 he did exactly that. As late as 1996, Boris Becker's name would be attached to a grand slam triumph when he won the Australian Open.

1980 1981 1982 1983 1984 **1985** 1986 1987 1988 1989

Above: Boris Becker celebrates winning the Men's Singles Wimbledon final.

REMEMBER THE EIGHTIES

European team secures the Ryder Cup

The 1980s became the decade when European golfers were at last able to take on their American counterparts and beat them on a regular basis.

Up until this time, players from the USA had dominated all the major tournaments with the odd exception, and the Ryder Cup, competed for every two years by Great Britain and America, had become so predictably one-sided that there were suggestions of it becoming an event consigned to history.

To even up the contest, a decision was taken to turn the GB team into one that included Europeans. This was viewed by many as an indictment on the quality of British golfers but welcomed by others as a means of keeping the competition alive. The US still went into the 1985 contest with their usual confidence as they had already seen off the expanded European team on two

previous meetings during the decade, although in 1983 the margin had only been one point.

The scene was set for a close contest at the Belfry, but the final result came as a major shock to the US

Above: Sam Torrance celebrates with the Ryder Cup trophy after victory over the USA.
Below: The European Ryder Cup team.

team, who were beaten 16.5 to 11.5, the popular Scotsman Sam Torrance being the man who secured the winning point for the Europeans. The sight of non-playing captain Tony Jacklin (an Englishman who had occasionally rocked the American boat in the past) lifting the trophy after nearly three decades of US victories gladdened the hearts of all home supporters, who had reconciled themselves to never witnessing such an event. Perhaps a combined European team wasn't such a bad idea after all seemed to be the general consensus of opinion.

In subsequent years, the Ryder Cup has been fought for with great intensity, with emotion and sportsmanship occasionally taking a regrettable back seat.

POLITICS & CURRENT AFFAIRS

Gorbachev is Soviet leader

In March, the Soviet Union appointed Mikhail Gorbachev as head of the Communist party, whom everybody hoped would stay in the position longer than his two predecessors Chernenko and Andropov, both of whom died in office within 13 months of each other.

Gorbachev, as the youngest member of the Politburo at 54, looked more youthful than any previous Soviet leader and arrived with new ideas to boot. He obviously wanted a dialogue with the West and sought internal reforms totally alien to previous regimes.

1980 1981 1982 1983 1984 **1985** 1986 1987 1988 1989

Below: Mikhail Gorbachev and Ronald Reagan.

He had graduated from driving a harvester to a law degree from Moscow University in the post-Stalinist era. He arrived as a breath of fresh air heralding a new attitude in the Kremlin, a man the rest of the world could do business with but, by the decade's end, he would be struggling against opposition to his policies.

Josef Mengele is dead

During World War II, the Auschwitz concentration camp was home to one of the world's most reviled individuals. Dr Joseph Mengele, known as the 'Angel of Death', had carried out the most horrific experiments on the inmates, whose experiences either left them dead or traumatised. These experiments were purportedly conducted in the 'interests of science' but amounted to

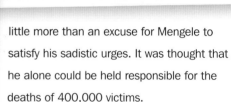

little more than an excuse for Mengele to satisfy his sadistic urges. It was thought that he alone could be held responsible for the deaths of 400,000 victims.

After the war, he slipped through the net that closed in on Nazi war criminals and disappeared to 'who knew where'. The most likely bolthole was South America where many of his fellow criminals had also absconded to. But he could never feel totally safe while he was alive for there were governments and organisations, many of them Jewish, ready to see him stand trial. The problem lay in pinning down his location.

Over nearly a 40-year period, Mengele stayed on the 'most wanted' list and whilst on occasions other Nazis were unearthed, he remained elusive. No proof existed that he had not died but the Nazi chasers would never

Above: Burned-out cars in the street the day after rioting on the Broadwater Farm Estate.
Below: German Nazi doctor and war criminal Josef Mengele.

1980 1981 1982 1983 1984 **1985** 1986 1987 1988 1989

give up whilst Mengele could still be at large.

In June, the mystery of Mengele was partly resolved when Brazilian police opened up a grave on the outskirts of Sao Paulo and took away the remains. After deliberation and use of updated scientific techniques, the announcement was made to the world that the experts were close to 100 per cent sure that they had found Mengele's body. After questioning, an Austrian couple admitted to having harboured him for no little time and his demise had come after a swimming accident.

Death of PC Keith Blakelock

A North London housing development, Broadwater Farm, which had been regarded as a model of its type, became the stage for one of the worst riots seen in the 1980s and proved that underlying tensions existed in the area. Although, animosity existed between the black community and the police, it was believed that the two could at least rub along together.

Inner city estates may have always had their problems but nobody could have predicted the event which made Broadwater Farm infamous. In the first week of October, hundreds of black youths rioted after a woman had died in her flat whilst the police were searching it. The reaction was extreme, to say the very least.

The police, carrying shields and batons, were met by stones, petrol bombs and simply any kind of missile the rioters could lay their hands on including concrete blocks hurled from the flats above. Cars were set on fire and the gravity of the situation became apparent when 40-year-old PC Keith Blakelock, well known in the vicinity, was hacked to death. The local police simply could not cope and many others were drafted in from various London boroughs. For the first time ever the Metropolitan Police tactical firearms squad found themselves on the streets, the situation was clearly critical.

A PC took a blast from a revolver full in the stomach and three other policemen felt the effects of shotgun fire. By the end of the night over 200 policemen had been injured.

Three men were charged with the murder of PC Blakelock, the most well-known being Winston Silcott. Upon appeal all three were cleared of the crime, although Silcott remained in prison for the murder of another man which he claimed had been in self-defence.

1980 1981 1982 1983 1984 **1985** 1986 1987 1988 1989

Below: PC Keith Blakelock.

1980 1981 1982 1983 1984 1985 1986 1987 1988 1989

1986

FASHION, CULTURE & ENTERTAINMENT

Phantom of the Opera opens

First published as a novel by Gaston Leroux in France in 1910, musical maestro Andrew Lloyd Webber's adaptation of *The Phantom Of The Opera* opened to rave reviews at London's Her Majesty's Theatre on 9 October 1986 and continues to delight theatre-goers today. There have been lengthy debates as to whether the story is

based on true events – as the author claimed – or not, but no concrete evidence has ever been produced.

Starring comic actor Michael Crawford as the Phantom, the former *Some Mothers Do 'Ave 'Em* star astounded audiences with his singing voice, particularly on 'Music Of The Night'. He again played the title role when the musical opened on Broadway a year later and his co-stars in the original production – Lloyd Webber's wife of two years Sarah Brightman and Steve Barton – also made the transition from London to New York.

Phantom Of The Opera is a love triangle between the main characters: Christine,

Above: Michael Crawford and Sarah Brightman.
Below: Poster for 'The Phantom of the Opera' film released in 2004.

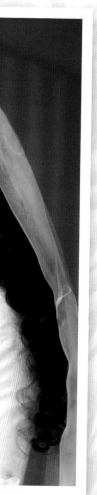

Raoul (the Vicompte de Chagney) and the Phantom (originally called Erik in the novel but not named at any stage in the musical). Christine, a chorus girl at the Paris Opera House in the late nineteenth century, has suffered since the death of her father and gets help with her singing from a mysterious voice in her dressing room. On realising that she has fallen in love with her childhood friend Raoul, the Phantom – a brilliant composer and musician who wears a mask to hide the facial disfiguration he has had to bear since birth – makes himself known to her and leads her down to the cellars, where he has made his home, to try to win her heart.

A 1989 film was made of the book, starring Robert Englund, but it would not be until 2004 that a version was made based on the musical itself.

Virginia Andrews dies

After a struggle against breast cancer, international best-selling author Virginia C Andrews died on 19 December 1986 and was buried in her birthplace of Portsmouth, Virginia.

Cleo Virginia Andrews, born on 6 June 1923, was the youngest of three children and suffered a tragic accident during her teenage years, hurting her back after falling down stairs. A failed surgical attempt to rectify her injury, coupled with

arthritis, left her having to use crutches or a wheelchair for most of her life.

Disillusioned with her career as a fashion illustrator and commercial artist, she turned her hand to writing and submitted her first novel, *The Gods Of The Green Mountain*, in 1972, which was never published. Undaunted, she continued her efforts and eventually gained acclaim for her controversial 1979 novel *Flowers In The Attic* that explored child abuse, neglect and incest. This was the first in her Dollanganger series of novels and was made into a film in 1987.

The sequel, *Petals On The Wind*, surfaced the following year and within two years these two titles alone had sold seven million copies. The remaining three books in the series were published between 1981-86.

With more than 60 synopses written for future titles at the time of her death, Andrews' estate decided to hire a ghost writer to bring these ideas to life. Their identity was a closely kept secret at first but it has since emerged that Andrew Neiderman is the person behind the continuing publications and, while most agree that he is doing a reasonable job at imitating her style, all are of the opinion that the new novels would have been better if Andrews herself had been alive to complete the writing.

Two books of the Casteel series were published in Andrews' lifetime and she started on the other three but it was left to Neiderman to complete the unfinished manuscripts.

1980 1981 1982 1983 1984 1985 **1986** 1987 1988 1989

Above and below: 'Flowers in the Attic' film on DVD and 'Petals on the Wind' book.

1989 1988 1987 **1986** 1985 1984 1983 1982 1981 1980

such as boxer briefs, gripper boxers and yoke-front boxers and they are still just as, if not more, popular more than 20 years later with designer labels such as Gucci, Calvin Klein, Hugo Boss and Armani all getting in on the act.

Single-use camera

Fujifilm introduced the single-use 'Quicksnap' camera to

Boxer shorts

The big fashion hit of 1986 for men were boxer shorts. Popularised by a Levi's advert the previous year after the censor board had decreed that Y-fronts were indecent, every respectable man was trying out the new underwear and ditching their Y-fronts. The advert had starred model and singer Nick Kamen stripping down to his boxers in a launderette to wash his jeans, accompanied by Marvin Gaye's 'I Heard It Through The Grapevine'.

The origins of boxer shorts can be traced back to 1925, when Elastoplast founder Jacob Golumb created a new pair of shorts with an elasticated waist for boxers to wear while fighting…hence the name! There are now different types of boxers

Above: Y Fronts which were once considered indecent are now outdated.
Below: Nick Kamen who popularised boxers after appearing in an advert.

REMEMBER THE EIGHTIES

can be taken into situations where you wouldn't want to risk an expensive outfit.

Casio keyboard

With the increasing popularity of Electropop and sampling in the late 1970s and early 1980s it was no surprise when electronics giant Casio launched their SK1 sampler keyboard aimed primarily at the home toy market.

Marketed as a 'polyphonic digital sampling machine', its limited memory meant you could capture a two-minute

the public in 1986. This jointly invented camera by Fujifilm and Kodak meant the whole camera was handed over for the film to be processed. In an attempt to promote recycling awareness the unit could be reloaded with film and then sold to the next budding David Bailey.

Other major manufacturers such as Nikon, Konica and Canon soon launched their own versions. In an effort to remain the market leaders, Fujifilm gave their cameras added extras such as panoramic views, built-in flash and even produced a unit that can be used underwater.

Single-use cameras with focus free lenses soon became very popular as they are inexpensive compared to a real camera, they are easily used by children and

sample and it also boasted a built-in microphone plus 13 sound envelopes to turn even the most unknowledgeable person into a *real* musician. There were also preset PCM samples – piano, brass ensemble, trumpet, synth drum and human voice – that you could add to your tune.

The major disadvantage to owning a SK1 was that, once you had programmed all this into your keyboard, it was lost as soon as you switched the power off! It has, however, been reportedly favoured by such luminaries as Blur, Fatboy Slim and Portishead.

Above: Fuji disposable cameras and film on sale in Japan.
Below: The Casio SK1 keyboard.

MUSIC

January

Phil Lynott, former leader of Thin Lizzy, passed away on 4 January 1986 in Salisbury Infirmary, suffering a complete system failure after a heroin overdose on Christmas Day 1985. He had been battling heroin and alcohol dependency for the last years of his life.

Lynott was born in West Bromwich on 20 August 1949 of a black Brazilian father and Irish Catholic mother, Philomena (Phyllis). When his father left shortly afterwards, his mother returned to Dublin where Phil was brought up.

The band had a hit with 'Whiskey in the Jar' in 1973 but their career really took off three years later with the single 'The Boys Are Back In Town' and album 'Live and Dangerous', acclaimed as one of the best live records ever.

In 1980, Lynott married Caroline, daughter of comedian Leslie Crowther, also launching a parallel solo career in that year. Thin Lizzy disbanded in the mid-1980s.

The first inductions to the newly-established Rock and Roll Hall of Fame took place this month. Although the ceremonies are held in New York City, the organisation's headquarters and museum is situated on

Below: Phil Lynott in concert shortly before his death.

REMEMBER THE EIGHTIES

are only eligible for induction twenty-five years after the release of their first recordings. Each inductee has a dedicated exhibit in the museum.

The Rock and Roll Hall of Fame was the brainchild of former *Rolling Stone* editor Jann Wenner and music writer Dave Marsh. Inductees are selected by committees comprised of journalists, producers and other music business luminaries. Although ostensibly international in its scope, the Hall of Fame has been largely dominated by American and British acts. Criticisms have been levelled at the choice of inductees; some artists of questionable relevance have been included whilst entire genres such as progressive rock, heavy metal and dance music have so far been ignored. The only act to refuse to attend the induction ceremony

the shores of Lake Eyrie in Cleveland, Ohio. The city was chosen as the site for the Hall of Fame because one of its native sons, disc jockey Alan Freed, was an early champion of the music and is generally acknowledged to have popularised the term "rock and roll".

The first inductees to the 'Performers' category were Chuck Berry, James Brown, Ray Charles, Fats Domino, Everly Brothers, Buddy Holly, Jerry Lee Lewis and Elvis Presley. The Hall of Fame also encompasses 'Non-performers' (songwriters, producers, disc jockeys, journalists), 'Early Influences' (artists from earlier eras) and, since 2000, 'Sidemen' (usually veteran session musicians). Artists

1980 1981 1982 1983 1984 1985 **1986** 1987 1988 1989

Above: Alan Freed who popularised the term 'rock and roll'.
Below: Elvis Presley, one of the early inductees in the Hall of Fame.

1980 1981 1982 1983 1984 1985 1986 1987 1988 1989

was the Sex Pistols who were inducted in their absence in 2006.

In November 2004, Britain launched its equivalent, the UK Music Hall of Fame. Amongst the founding members were The Beatles, Bob Marley and Madonna. Half of the inductees are voted for by the public each year.

July

Wham! played their last concert before a predominantly female audience of 80,000 at Wembley Stadium in July. Aptly dubbed *The Final*, the event featured special guest Elton John duetting with George Michael on 'Candle in the Wind'. The day was commemorated with a live album.

The split came as no surprise, although the group's record company Epic had denied it in March. Wham! was an unequal partnership with Michael shouldering the creative burden whilst guitarist Andrew Ridgeley, the singer's best friend, seemed to be along for the ride. George had already had one solo hit with 'Careless Whisper' the previous year and was planning a solo album for 1987.

Wham! were one of the decade's most successful outfits, becoming the first Western pop group to visit China. George Michael went on to make the potentially awkward transition from teen idol to serious

Below: Andrew Ridgeley and George Michael of Wham! performing on stage.

104

He renounced drugs after an American session musician was found dead at his Hampstead home in October, turning to Buddhism for solace. Boy George launched a solo career in 1987.

October

Two years after the last Pink Floyd album, 'The Final Cut', bassist and chief songwriter Roger Waters issued High Court proceedings aimed at preventing the remaining members from trading as Pink Floyd without him. Guitarist Dave Gilmour resolved to oppose

artist. Ridgeley married Bananarama's Keren Woodward and retired to Cornwall.

From his first appearances on *Top of the Pops* with Culture Club in 1982, Boy George was one of the 1980s' most recognisable pop stars. Culture Club achieved phenomenal worldwide success but by 1985, the hits had started to dry up and inter-band relationships soured, particularly that between the singer and his secret lover, drummer Jon Moss.

George turned to heroin and his brother went public with the news of his addiction in an effort to save him from the drug. He was hounded by the tabloids during the summer of 1986, describing himself as 'the world's most famous junkie' at an Artists Against Apartheid gig in July where he appeared in a jacket covered with stencilled obscenities in a vain attempt to thwart photographers.

Above: Culture Club.
Below: Boy George outside his London home talking about giving up drugs in 1986.

1980 1981 1982 1983 1984 1985 **1986** 1987 1988 1989

1980 1981 1982 1983 1984 1985 **1986** 1987 1988 1989

him. 'He left and we wanted to carry on with our careers. It's as simple as that.'

The dispute was eventually settled in December 1987 as Gilmour recalled. 'I met Roger to thrash out our... divorce. The two of us, one accountant, a computer and a printer. We hammered it out over a few hours, printed it and signed it. That's the legal document on money and rights we are bound by today. No shouting. We both wanted to get it sorted out.'

The war of words rumbled on. Waters described 'A Momentary Lapse of Reason', the first Floyd album without him as 'a very facile but quite clever forgery.' He was less impressed by 1994's 'The Division Bell',

commenting that he 'could not believe how awful it is – the songs are dreadful, all of them just awful. An awful, awful record.'

Pink Floyd had survived the departure of their original creative force Syd Barrett in 1968 and the brand prospered again twenty years on as the Gilmour-led outfit mounted a spectacular and successful world tour. Asked in 1990 whether he could envisage working with Waters again, Gilmour replied: 'I don't foresee it. He's done some terrible things. Honesty is not one of the things that he will let get in the way of his pursuit of power.'

In the summer of 2005, however, the two men were brought back together by Bob Geldof's legendary persuasive skills and the cause of

Below: David Gilmour with Kate Bush.
Middle: Pink Floyd with Roger Waters on microphone rehearsing prior to a concert.

Live 8. The vintage post-Barrett Pink Floyd line-up, completed by drummer Nick Mason and keyboardist Rick Wright, reunited for a memorable one-off performance in Hyde Park.

SPORT

Jahangir Khan loses World Title

In the world of squash, the Pakistani Jahangir Khan became a legend during his playing days and few people ever argued when he was dubbed the greatest player the world has seen.

Nobody believed that he could be beaten as he took his place in the November final against New Zealander Ross Norman, a good enough player perhaps but one who had failed to defeat Khan in over 30 attempts.

Everybody had automatically awarded the title to the Pakistani – after all he had not been defeated in over 500 matches going back in the excess of five and a half years.

The only person that stood between him and another title, looked like another lamb to the slaughter but Norman surpassed all expectations in the Toulouse final and took the honours by three games to one. Thus Norman became one of the great winning underdogs of the sporting 1980s.

Below: Jahangir Khan (right) plays Jansher Khan during a friendly match.

1980 1981 1982 1983 1984 1985 **1986** 1987 1988 1989

REMEMBER THE EIGHTIES

Argentina's World Cup win

At the end of June, Argentina led by Diego Maradona won the Mexico World Cup, beating West Germany 3-2 in the final. Having taken a 2-0 lead, the Argentineans let the Germans back into the game and only secured the win six minutes from time through a Burruchaga goal.

The countries had booked their places in the Final after both had won their semi-finals 2-0. West Germany had overcome France, probably the most talented team in the competition and Argentina had breezed past Belgium.

England's fortunes were ultimately mixed, starting with a disappointing 1-0 defeat against Portugal, the second game drawn 0-0 with Morocco and the final group game won 3-0 versus Poland thanks to a Gary Lineker hat-trick. Things seemed to be looking up and

Paraguay were dismissed 3-0 in the second round which booked a quarter-final game against Argentina.

The rest, as they say is history, as Maradona scored his 'hand of God' goal and added a magnificent second

Above: Diego Maradona of Argentina kisses the trophy after the World Cup Final.
Below: The 'hand of God' moment.

after a run from his own half. Lineker replied for England but they were out, beaten 2-1. This was the only quarter final game that achieved a result without going to a penalty shoot-out. England's consolation came from Gary Lineker being the top goal scorer in the tournament with six.

Scotland finished bottom of their group and took an early plane home. For a while in their game against West Germany they had clung to a 1-0 lead but eventually lost out. Northern Ireland finished second from the bottom in their group, failing to make the second round. They suffered defeats against Spain and Brazil, the one point they acquired coming from a 1-1 draw with Algeria.

The major talking point from the 1986 World Cup has always been Maradona's handled goal and lengthy debates regarding the incident were still taking place in the build-up to the 2006 event.

Mike Tyson youngest ever world heavyweight Champion

Las Vegas witnessed history in November when Mike Tyson, at the age of 20, became the youngest ever world heavyweight boxing champion. He had arrived at the fight for the WBC version of the title with a string of quick victories behind him and a reputation for unremitting aggression in the ring, not to say a degree of brutality. His young life on the tough streets of Brownsville, Brooklyn where he constantly courted trouble had prepared him well for the demanding life of a professional boxer which must have seemed reasonably

genteel compared to the environment he had been brought up in.

Despite Tyson's burgeoning profile, champion Trevor Berbick must have fancied his chances against his relatively inexperienced opponent. The champion's world soon turned upside-down however for the challenger's controlled assault from the opening minute undid him within two rounds and Tyson had claimed the title.

It was felt that Tyson would remain supreme in the heavyweight ranks for many years to come but due to a mixture of personal problems, imprisonment and accepting advice from those who should have known

Below: Mike Tyson listens to reporters during the weigh in for his fight against Trevor Berbick as promoter Don King looks on.

better, the champion was destined to become a reviled figure.

Unfortunately, he will be remembered as the man who bit off an opponent's ear (in the re-match against Evander Holyfield), as the man who went to prison and as a wife-beater, instead of being the outstanding fighter he undoubtedly was at his peak in the 1980s.

Tyson fought into the twenty-first century, when long past his best and no longer in prime condition. The money was prime consideration. He recorded a number of quick victories against journeymen fighters but failed miserably

when confronted by Lennox Lewis, who knocked him out in eight rounds. A defeat at the hands of the unknown Kevin McBride finished his career for good.

POLITICS & CURRENT AFFAIRS

Challenger explodes

The American space programme has always been dear to the hearts of US citizens, a matter of national pride and confirmation of their country's place in the world.

Below: The space shuttle Challenger takes off from the Kennedy Space Centre.

They believed the programme looked after its astronauts, who had often become national celebrities and despite the deaths of three individuals in 1967, after a freak launch-pad fire, they had come to believe it was safe. After all, men had been to the moon and back without much of a hitch.

In January, the space shuttle *Challenger* took off without sign of any problem, when suddenly the unimaginable happened. The spacecraft had risen only ten miles into the air, travelling at 2,000 mph, when a huge explosion took place killing the crew of six men and one woman. Within 73 seconds the future of America's space programme had been thrown into question and a nation horrified by the disaster. The take-off had been shown live on TV; a real-life drama that those who watched it will never forget.

The flight had been dogged by bad luck before take-off and delayed by close to a week, mainly due to inclement weather. But a little hardware problem also came along to frustrate the situation even further. The craft even had to be cleared of icicles not long before launch time, as the temperature the night before had fallen well below zero.

Many theories were put forward as to the cause of the tragedy, freezing temperatures the night before being just one of them, but it took an official NASA enquiry to come to a firm conclusion. Apparently, the explosion of the fuel tank had been prompted by a sequence of failures put into motion by a faulty seal on a rocket booster.

Above: An abstract smoke pattern after the space shuttle Challenger explosion.

1989 1988 1987 1986 1985 1984 1983 1982 1981 1980

Marcos flees Manila

Three years after her husband had been killed by the forces of Ferdinand Marcos, Corazon Aquino was installed as president of the Philippines in February, shortly after Ferdinand, Imelda and family had beaten a hasty exit from the capital Manila.

On 7 February, Marcos had announced his victory in an election which had been rigged in his favour. It was at this point that world opinion turned against him, and the United States, which had backed him long-term, started to hedge its bets.

This signalled the beginning of the end for the dictatorial Marcos. The strong men in the army also decided his time had come, making a significant move in taking over the Defence Ministry.

The people took the final decision when they attacked the Malacanang Palace, forcing the

Marcos family to take to the roof, from which they were plucked at the eleventh hour by US helicopters.

Chernobyl disaster

In April, a disaster struck the Chernobyl power station some 80 miles north of Kiev, which promised to have catastrophic effects on the surrounding area for years to come. The Soviet Union were slow to issue the true facts of the matter, until they were forced into making a statement after high radiation levels were recorded elsewhere in Europe.

It was revealed that one of the reactors (number four to be exact) at the Ukrainian located plant had blown its top off, after basic safety measures had been ignored during routine safety checks. The other three reactors were shut down instantly. The blazing reactor caused immediate problems for local experts and slowly requests emerged for assistance from other countries to contain the conflagration. Initially, the International Atomic Energy Agency refused to help.

First reports indicated that only two people had been killed instantly by the explosion but when the truth emerged the

Above: President Marcos declares that the country is in a state of emergency.
Below: Ferdinand Marcos, his wife Imelda and his Vice President Arturo Tolentino celebrate for victory at the elections.

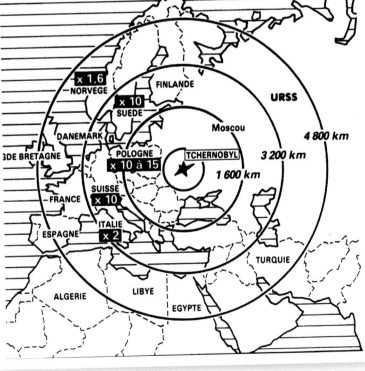

figure rose to 30. A total of some 135,000 people were evacuated from within a 20-mile radius of the plant, as the fear of radiation grew. In the West, reactors have secondary protection to contain radioactive fall-out but in the mid-1980s the Soviet Union lacked such basic safety measures.

In the days after the accident, doubts still existed as to how safe the plant remained, although the Soviet authorities made many reassurances to the effect that things were under control. Further deaths occurred and instances of cancer became apparent. Chernobyl became a tainted ghost town.

In the twenty-first century, the Chernobyl situation still exists as a cause for concern, with high radiation levels being ignored by locals who had returned to the location. A UN report appeared to talk down the imminent danger but frequent news items suggested an extremely unhealthy environment.

Above and below: Repairs being carried out on the Chernobyl nuclear plant after the explosion and a map illustrating the areas affected by the explosion at Chernobyl.

1980 1981 1982 1983 1984 1985 1986 **1987** 1988 1989

1987

FASHION, CULTURE & ENTERTAINMENT

Dirty Dancing

On 1 January 1987, Emile Ardolino's *Dirty Dancing* hit the American big screen. Written by Eleanor Bergstein, the film tells the story of Frances (Baby) Houseman and her trip to a family holiday resort, Kellerman's, with her family in 1963. As a tale of morals, love, romance and of course, dancing, it went on to win several major awards including an

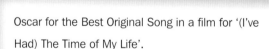

Oscar for the Best Original Song in a film for '(I've Had) The Time of My Life'.

Known to family and friends as Baby, Frances (Jennifer Grey) is a young woman on the verge of adulthood. She is inquisitive and after falling in love with dance teacher Johnny Castle – played by Patrick Swayze – finds herself drawn to his world away from the dance floor. What she discovers is a new dance craze called 'dirty dancing' which in the early 1960s was frowned upon by older generations.

When Johnny's hopes of winning a local dance contest with friend Penny are dashed when it's discovered she's pregnant and has an abortion, Baby persuades Johnny to teach her how to dance

Above: Dancers rehearse for the world premiere of the 'Dirty Dancing' stage production.
Below: Patrick Swayze and Jennifer Grey, co-stars of 'Dirty Dancing'.

office hits such as *Roadhouse* (1989), the perennial weepy *Ghost* (the film of 1990) and *Point Break* with Keanu Reeves (1991).

Smileys-Acid House

The year of 1987 saw the explosion of Acid House music in the clubs around Britain that paved the way for the raves – both legal and illegal – that would follow. It had evolved from House music and added squelch and a deep bassline from a Roland TB303 machine.

The source of the name is a constant topic of debate, some thinking it relates to the drug culture while others believe it to have originated from the first single to be classified as Acid House, 'Acid Trax' by Phuture. One thing everyone is agreed upon, however, is that it all started in Chicago.

The genre used samplers to take existing excerpts of different music and merge them together with a drum beat and vocals to produce a new song, and some of the better known Acid House artists to hit the big time were the KLF (also known as the Justified Ancients of Mu Mu), 808 State and the Shamen. They later consolidated the media's attention on the drug

and a relationship blossoms. The film deals with various attitudes of the time, responsibility and emotions. Grey manages to portray every experience that Baby faces with such realism while Swayze gives Johnny's character a strong personality with appeal and depth.

The success of the movie can largely be credited to both Grey and Swayze whose chemistry on screen is enchanting and powerful despite the plot's predictability. Other successful ingredients to the film were the music and songs that accompanied the sensual dancing.

This was the film that really launched Patrick Swayze's career and he went on to star in box

1980 1981 1982 1983 1984 1985 1986 **1987** 1988 1989

Below: Four differently styled Smiley badges.

affiliation with their 'Ebeneezer Goode' single with its chorus that sounded like they were singing 'Es are good' (E being a nickname for Ecstasy).

The Smiley, a yellow button with two eyes and a smiling mouth, became the symbol of Acid House and is alleged to have first been associated with the music when DJ Danny Rampling returned from Ibiza and used the logo on one of his flyers.

In truth, the Smiley has been around a lot longer than that with the first recorded usage of the yellow face being in 1963 when Harvey Ball created it for State Mutual Life Assurance in Massachusetts. Unfortunately, the patent of the logo did not get approval before it fell into the public domain. Emoticon smileys – :-) – and its counterpart frowneys – :-(– are now commonly used in text messaging and emailing.

Cycling shorts

One of the trends of 1987 that was only kind to those with an athletic figure were the cycling shorts. Designed for cyclists to wear while riding to provide more comfort, ease the build up of perspiration, prevent chafing and decrease wind resistance, the original shorts were made of black wool and leather chamois but manufacturing techniques changed with the arrival of new technology.

These shorts were made of Lycra and came in a variety of colours, some traditional with many more sporting gaudy designs. The way the Lycra gave the shorts

Above: Linford Christie with his cycling shorts inspired althletic suit.

a tight, supportive fit was also designed to help the quadriceps muscle in the thigh, one of the weakest muscles in the human body.

It was not just cyclists who took to wearing cycling shorts in their chosen sports, though, as many footballers chose them to wear under their normal shorts as an alternative to the jockstrap.

Nike Air trainers

Nike launched their Air Max shoe in 1987, the first of many versions of that branded footwear that have since proved the brilliance of the idea. The shoe was revolutionary in using a visible large cushioning unit in the sole. For the first and only time, a Beatles track – 'Revolution' – was used in a television commercial to promote the product.

The technology had been the brainchild of inventor M Frank Rudy and he patented the idea in 1979. The concept was simple: gas-filled plastic pockets are

inserted into the sole during manufacturing to provide cushioning for the runner's feet.

Nike, named after the Greek goddess of victory, had been formed 15

years earlier by coach Bill Bowerman and middle-distance runner Phil Knight who had spent much of the previous decade supplying shoes that had been made by third parties.

Karaoke

Karaoke first became popular with businessmen in Japan who used to pop into a bar on the way home and belt out their favourite hits. The term karaoke is derived from the Japanese words kara(ppo) meaning empty and oke(sutura) meaning orchestra.

It is alleged that the craze began when a guitarist failed to turn up for a gig at a bar in Kobe City so the owner prepared accompaniment tapes for patrons to sing along to. Nowadays, karaoke is rife in the UK with bars in every city and town hosting evenings where drunken punters can sing along to backing tracks – such as Whitney Houston's 'I Will Always Love You' and Frank Sinatra's 'New York, New York' – while reading the lyrics on a TV screen.

There have even been mass-produced machines manufactured for home entertainment, an indication of how popular karaoke has become over the last 20 years.

1980 1981 1982 1983 1984 1985 1986 **1987** 1988 1989

Middle: Nike Air trainers in action.
Below: A Japanese lady singing karaoke.

1980 1981 1982 1983 1984 1985 1986 **1987** 1988 1989

MUSIC

January

Launched in 1983, the compact disc was initially regarded as a medium for hi-fi enthusiasts only. CD eventually superseded vinyl, but this was a gradual process, a vital stage of which was reached in January 1987 when the first four Beatles albums became available on CD, accompanied by a marketing campaign aimed at securing a massive increase of sales of both discs and players.

The only previous appearance of Beatles music in the new format occurred when Toshiba Japan pressed some copies of 'Abbey Road' before being instructed to desist by EMI. The delay in transferring the most successful back catalogue in rock history led to rumours, strenuously denied by the company, that EMI did not own the CD rights to the Beatles' music.

The Fab Four's remaining albums were re-issued during the year, with the CD version of 'Sergeant Pepper' coinciding with the twentieth anniversary of its original release on 1 June 1967.

March

After their remarkable performance at Live Aid, expectations were high for U2's next album and 'The Joshua Tree', unleashed in March 1987, did not disappoint. The band's career had been steadily gaining momentum from their post-punk origins in Dublin. The predecessor to 'The Joshua Tree', 'The Unforgettable Fire', also produced by Brian Eno and Daniel Lanois, was a crucial point in U2's evolution, demonstrating a new maturity both in song-writing and execution.

Below: The Beatles albums are released on CD.

the microphone. The album's success both in the UK and America saw U2 graduate into their natural environment as stadium fillers. Shortly after its release, the foursome were featured on the cover of America's *Time* magazine – only the third rock band, after the Beatles and the Who, to receive that accolade.

The phenomenally successful writing and production team of Stock, Aitken and Waterman were at the summit of the charts in March 1987 with Mel and Kim's 'Respectable'. This was replaced at the top by their production of the Ferry Aid charity record, a version of the Beatles' 'Let It Be'. SAW were also behind the year's biggest-selling single, Rick Astley's 'Never Gonna Give You Up'.

1980 1981 1982 1983 1984 1985 1986 **1987** 1988 1989

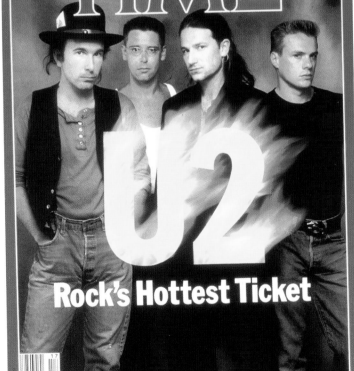

The band's fifth studio album, 'The Joshua Tree' added a widescreen element to the band's anthemic songs. For the first time, Bono's lyrics were composed in advance rather than at

119

Middle: Bono, lead singer of U2 in concert.
Below: Time cover featuring U2.

1980 1981 1982 1983 1984 1985 1986 **1987** 1988 1989

Matt Stock, Mike Aitken and Pete Waterman joined forces in 1984, scoring their first hit with Divine's 'You'll Never Be A Man' in that year, followed quickly by Hazell Dean's 'Whatever I Do'. Their production of Dead or Alive's 'You Spin Me Round (Like A Record)' went to Number 1 in March 1985 but the trio were struggling financially. This prompted a change in direction away from the frantic Hi-NRG sound to a bubblegum pop style which brought greater rewards but also much derision. 'I regret that we're so disliked by our peers,' complained Waterman, who defended their production-line output by comparing it to Tamla Motown.

Waterman described how the partnership worked in the studio. 'The musicians are Matt and Mike. Mike's the songwriter. We write the lyrics between the three of us while we're actually making the songs.'

Despite Waterman's claim that 'We've always been backroom boys, that's all we've ever wanted to be,' the trio became household words and they enjoyed several hits in their own right, beginning with the largely instrumental 'Roadblock'. This became the subject of legal proceedings because of the use of unauthorised samples on 'Pump Up The Volume' by M/A/R/R/S.

Above: Rick Astley performing on stage.

REMEMBER THE EIGHTIES

In 1988, the trio were back at Number 1 with 'I Should Be So Lucky', sung by Kylie Minogue, then a relatively-unknown actress on the Australian soap opera *Neighbours*. Stock, Aitken and Waterman were responsible for 141 UK hit singles over a ten-year period.

August

The curtain came down on the turbulent five-year career of the Smiths this month when guitarist Johnny Marr announced that he had quit the

Mancunian outfit. A number of factors lay behind the decision but essentially Marr had become disenchanted. 'The one thing about a group who create a certain style and create a certain political aspect to what they do, it gets to be a club. And some things are in and some things are out,' he explained. 'Towards the end of the Smiths, I realised that the records I was listening to with my friends were more exciting than the records I was listening to with the group. Eventually we'd got ourselves down a musical and political cul-de-sac.'

Lead singer Morrissey was shocked by his songwriting partner's defection. 'I felt completely betrayed because the Smiths were a tremendous emotional investment. I'd given so much of myself to the group, and suddenly, by a stupid whim, everything was spoilt. I found it so unfair.' Morrissey tentatively tried to keep the Smiths alive by bringing

Above: Kylie Minogue.
Below: Songwriting trio Stock, Aitken and Waterman.

1980 1981 1982 1983 1984 1985 1986 **1987** 1988 1989

in guitarist Ivor Perry to rehearse with drummer Mike Joyce and bassist Andy Rourke but quickly thought better of it and instead opted for a solo career.

For most of their lifetime, the Smiths had operated without a manager. During their final American tour in 1987, much of the burden of management tasks was falling on Johnny Marr, putting an intolerable strain on the 23-year-old guitarist. Marr became something of a guitarist-for-hire, playing with Bryan Ferry, the Pretenders and The The, before forming the Healers in the late 1990s

The Smiths were about to leave independent label Rough Trade, following several disputes, to record with major EMI. Their final album, 'Strangeways, Here We Come' was released posthumously in October 1987.

December

The Pogues, who combined punk energy and traditional Irish music, had not troubled the Top Ten previously and were unlikely contenders for the 1987 Christmas Number 1. In the event, they were stranded in second place behind the Pet Shop Boys' version of 'Always On My Mind'. Despite this apparent setback, 'Fairytale of New York' has gone on to be widely acclaimed as the greatest Christmas single ever, twice winning polls to that effect carried out by the music video channel VH-1.

Taking its title from a JP Donleavy novel, 'Fairytale' was a year in gestation, originating in the opening piano refrain by co-composer Jem Finer before the lyrics were added by Pogues frontman Shane MacGowan. Kirsty MacColl was not originally to have been featured. She contributed a guide vocal at the request of her husband, Pogues producer Steve Lilywhite, which the band liked so much that they asked her to sing on the final version.

SPORT

All Blacks win first ever Rugby Union World Cup

Even though there were doubts in some quarters about their ability to take the World Cup on home turf, the New Zealand All Blacks duly obliged with a 29-9 victory over France. No mean achievement, as the French side contained

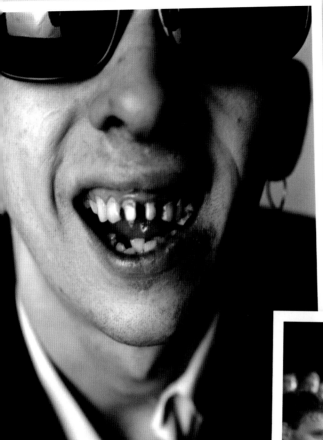

The final turned out to be something of a damp squib, the French unable to play their normal expansive running game and New Zealand going for safety first rather than heroics. Grant Fox, the All Black fly-half, scored 17 points made up of 4 penalties and a conversion, the home side's tries came from Michael Jones, the great John Kirwan and captain/scrum half David Kirk. Pierre Berbizier scored France's only try and Camberabero kicked the rest.

These were the days of the amateur and the often told story of New Zealand full-back John Gallagher returning to his job as a policeman the following day typified the lot of an international rugby player in the 1980s.

outstanding backs in Serge Blanco, Pierre Berbizier, Didier Camberabero and Philippe Sella.

France entered the game after a thrilling semi-final victory over Australia, which took its toll on the players and left them under par for the greatest game of their lives. On the other hand New Zealand had a relative stroll in their semi, brushing aside Wales 49-6. The Welsh had taken great heart from their quarter-final victory over England but failed to match the All Blacks in any department. Scotland had also made it beyond the first stage but fallen to the All Blacks 30-3.

1980 1981 1982 1983 1984 1985 1986 **1987** 1988 1989

Above: Shane MacGowan of the Pogues.
Below: David Kirk, captain of New Zealand, holds the Rugby World Cup trophy.

1980 1981 1982 1983 1984 1985 1986 **1987** 1988 1989

The All Black success heralded a sequence of World Cup wins for southern hemisphere country teams which eventually came to an end when England took the trophy in 2003, finally putting to bed the theory that a northern hemisphere was unlikely ever to win the competition.

Stephen Roche's Tour De France victory

In July, Ireland's Stephen Roche claimed victory in the world's most famous cycle race, the Tour De France, in the process becoming only the second man outside continental Europe to taste success in this gruelling event. Greg Lemond from the USA had broken the stranglehold the previous year but Roche's triumph carried further satisfaction as he had long played second fiddle to his fellow countryman Sean Kelly.

Roche left it fairly late to secure his win, only securing the yellow jersey after beating Pedro Delgado to the punch in the penultimate day's time trial. The

Below: Stephen Roche in action in the Tour de France.

124

to come their way in the fourth World Cup held in India and Pakistan.

Both host countries reached the semi-finals, where their interest in the tournament ended as Australia beat Pakistan, and England, thanks to a century from Graham Gooch, put paid to India. The big disappointment came in the failure of the West Indies to make any kind of impact.

The final played at Eden Gardens in Calcutta, predicted to be close, was exactly that with Australia running out winners by only seven runs. Captain Allan Border had 'man of the match' David Boon with his 75 runs to thank for victory.

40-second advantage he gained may have looked slim but proved to be enough as he unobtrusively arrived in the Champs Elysées as part of the main pack. His unashamed joy as he crossed the line must have been balanced by a fair amount of relief. Roche's hour had arrived and surely carried more weight than Delgado's drug-tainted victory the following year.

More trials and tribulations for English cricket

After the controversy of the rebel tour earlier in the decade and the 'blackwash' at the hands of the West Indies in 1984, English cricket was looking for some kind of success

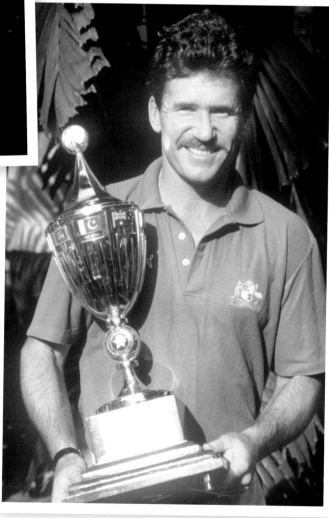

1980 1981 1982 1983 1984 1985 1986 **1987** 1988 1989

Above: Calcutta cricket ground during the final of the World Cup between England and Australia.
Below: Allan Border poses with the World Cup after his team won the final.

So England moved on with a tour of Pakistan which became infamous for a single incident which probably had its roots in increasingly bad blood between the two sides that had festered away for a number of years.

In the Faisalabad Test played in December, the second day was in its last over when England captain Mike Gatting became involved in a heated argument over the movement of a fielder which umpire Shakoor Rana objected to. Within seconds the two were nose-to-nose, finger wagging and looking close to fisticuffs.

Much was made of who should apologise to whom and a whole day's play was lost as fallout from the incident started to involve other personalities, including the Pakistani stand-in captain Javed Miandad who reportedly poured a little oil on already troubled waters. A truce was eventually arrived at and the match drawn, the cricket almost becoming a sideshow to the main event.

POLITICS & CURRENT AFFAIRS

Kidnap of Terry Waite

In January, Terry Waite, the Archbishop of Canterbury's special envoy, disappeared in Beirut whilst on a mission to negotiate the release of hostages held by Islamic militants. At first, observers declared that as he preferred to keep a low profile, he had chosen to take himself off alone because he felt negotiations had reached a stage where a little behind the scenes tinkering would benefit the situation.

Waite had been under the protection of Druze militia, whom he had insisted should allow him a little leeway in his quest. Without back-up from his guards, led by Walid Jumblatt, Waite was clearly vulnerable and, after failing to return to his hotel after a night time foray, alarm bells were ringing. Though he had denied connections to the Irangate crisis in some quarters his being taken as a hostage would have been perfectly plausible.

Jumblatt put out feelers, hoping to receive positive news but fearing the worst. Finally, an offshoot of Islamic Jihad, called Shia Amal, laid claim to having taken Waite as a prisoner whose return was non-negotiable – and so began an ordeal which lasted nearly five years.

For four of those years nobody knew whether he was still alive, his wife and four children back in Blackheath living on a permanent knife edge.

Below: Shakoor Rana the Pakistani umpire (left) with Mike Gatting of England and team manager Peter Lush during the controversial bust up over ball tampering in the test match against Pakistan.

and the luxury of a radio had only been allowed towards the end of his incarceration.

Stock market crash

What came to be known as 'Black Monday' caught monetary experts unawares and, on 19 October, ten per cent of the value of the stock market disappeared in one day, leaving both experienced and uninitiated dealers reeling from the shock.

The London market took a battering from 7 a.m. until close of play as to sell seemed the only order of the day. It emerged as the blackest day on the stock market for a century.

Markets around the world also suffered, as Wall Street performed even worse than its London counterpart, recalling memories of the late 1920s crash. Tokyo experienced similar jitters and Hong Kong took the drastic measure of closing its doors for a week.

Only when Brian Keenan and subsequently John McCarthy were released in the early-1990s did the news arrive of his survival, albeit in the most horrendous of conditions. McCarthy had been released in August 1991 when the picture on hostage release looked brighter and three months later, the stoical Waite also arrived home. During his captivity, much of the time chained to a wall, his only verbal contact had been with his guards

Above: Terry Waite on the Beirut seafront surrounded by heavily armed bodyguards.
Below: Front page of 'The Philadelphia Inquirer' the day of the stock market crash, October 20 1987.

REMEMBER THE EIGHTIES

On the evening of 15 October, on air BBC weatherman Michael Fish jovially rejected a claim from a caller who believed a hurricane was on its way. His assurances to the contrary were literally blown away hours later when recorded winds up to a speed of 110 mph laid waste to a huge swathe of England.

The reasons for the economic meltdown were various in nature and confidence was soon restored to the business world, but 'Black Monday' is a nightmare than can always potentially return.

Hurricane-force winds hit the south of England less than a handful of days before the stock market crash, the south of England experienced some crashing (and banging) of its own as exceptionally strong winds wreaked havoc across an area running from Cornwall up into East Anglia. After the event, weather experts declared that whilst the winds were hurricane force, the conditions did not match those of a fully-fledged hurricane, which made little difference to the people whose towns and property took the full brunt of the storm.

Above: The market appears to be too much for this trader as stocks were devastated on one of the most frantic days in the history of Wall Street.
Below: A policeman surveys the storm damage on a London road.

REMEMBER THE EIGHTIES

Those who had miraculously slept through the storm of the century woke in amazement at the scene of devastation. Roads and railway lines were blocked by fallen trees, thousands of homes had no electricity and a number of unfortunates had been killed. Commuters almost without exception found their journey to work disrupted or totally impossible.

The London fire brigade found themselves stretched beyond capacity, having to deal with thousands of emergency calls. One third of the trees at Kew Gardens came down and emergency departments in hospitals filled with victims of flying debris. The background noise to so many people's lives for days afterwards proved to be the whirring of electric saws cutting into wood, strewn across streets, gardens and parks. It would take some considerable time before electricity was totally restored to all the homes affected.

Caught with its pants down on this occasion, the Meteorological Office has had a tendency ever since to overstate the case when bad weather is potentially imminent.

1980 1981 1982 1983 1984 1985 1986 **1987** 1988 1989

Above: Storm damage in Soho Square, London.
Below: Michael Fish who famously failed to forecast the hurricane.

1980 1981 1982 1983 1984 1985 1986 1987 **1988** 1989

1988

FASHION, CULTURE & ENTERTAINMENT

Kenneth Williams dies

The world of comedy lost a legend on 15 April 1988 when *Carry On* star Kenneth Williams was found dead in his flat by his mother, who had let herself in after her son did not show up for an arranged meeting. The coroner recorded an open verdict after a lethal cocktail of sleeping pills and painkillers were detected in his system. Williams – a noted hypochondriac – had been suffering from a stomach ulcer and suicide was considered possible but unlikely in the official report although the last entry in his diary indicates that the pain was tortuous finishing with 'Oh – what's the bloody point.'

Williams, born in London on 22 February 1926, found his father did not approve of his acting ambitions and wanted him to put his drawing skills to use as a draughtsman before the Second World War intervened and he was conscripted into the Army.

Below: The actor and comedian Kenneth Williams.

REMEMBER THE EIGHTIES

His first big screen performance was in Laurence Olivier's film *The Beggar's Opera* but, to his horror, his voice was later dubbed by another actor who sounded more Cockney! His first big break was being asked to join the *Hancock's Half Hour* radio series in 1954 before he joined forces with Kenneth Horne four years later for Beyond Our Ken and its sequel *Round The Horne.*

Never completely happy in the theatre – he would get bored doing the same show day in day out – Williams found a niche in comedy and went on to star in 26 *Carry On...* films between 1958-78. With his ability to create different voices, he was also a regular reader on children's story programme *Jackanory* and narrated the *Willo The Wisp* television series in the early 1980s.

In March 2006, *Fantabulosa!* – a drama of his life starring Michael Sheen – gave BBC Four their highest ever viewing figures of nearly one million.

Bros/Brosettes

The biggest pop sensation in 1988 was Bros, a trio from Peckham, London, who took the music world by storm with their single 'When Will I Be Famous', a massive Number 2 hit. Their debut single 'I Owe You Nothing' had failed to chart the previous year but was re-released to give the boys their first UK Number 1 later in 1988.

Bros consisted of blonde twins Luke and Matt Goss together with school-friend Craig Logan, who was ousted from the band by the end of the year. He later sued the Goss twins for unpaid royalties and was awarded £1 million in compensation.

By the time Bros disbanded in 1992, they had racked up an impressive 11 Top 40 singles and three hit albums. They were also involved with Band Aid II, lending their vocal talents to the remake of 'Do They Know It's Christmas?' in 1989.

Wearing mascara and lip gloss, Bros appealed to hordes of young teenage girls who designed their own fashion. Nicknamed 'Brosettes', their 'uniform' consisted of ripped jeans, Doc Marten's boots with a Grolsch lager bottle top attached to the laces and black puffa jackets with the Bros logo on the back. It is reported that some of these fans took things to the extreme, pretending to faint outside the family home in Peckham in an attempt to get their idols' attention.

Both Matt and Luke have tried launching solo careers with little success. Luke has also tried to establish himself as an actor, with roles in *Blade II* and *The Man* on the big screen and as Danny in a West End adaptation of the musical *Grease*. Craig Logan currently lives in the States and manages pop

Below: Bros, consisting of Craig Logan (left) and twin brothers Matt and Luke Goss.

star Pink while heading up Sony BMG's RCA Records label.

Barbour jackets

Just like the rise in popularity of the 4x4 vehicle as an everyday means of transport, so another countryside icon found itself in the city during 1988. The Barbour jacket was created to protect farmers from the elements but was appropriated by office workers more accustomed to wielding umbrellas than pitchforks.

The company had been formed by John Barbour, the son of a Scottish farmer in Galloway, who began selling oilskins to fishermen and sailors in South Shields in 1894; the business evolved from there.

The Barbour jacket is manufactured from oiled Egyptian cotton, is very durable and is extremely waterproof and windproof. With regular reproofing, these jackets have been known to last up to 50 years. They have been worn by the military and have proved extremely popular with motorcyclists, with nearly every British international team from 1936-77 wearing an all-in-one suit made from the material.

Football inflatables

Although the first recorded appearance of a giant inflatable banana on the Maine Road terraces was in the summer of 1987, the 1988-89 season will be remembered as the time when the craze really took off.

When Manchester City visited West Bromwich Albion, fans tried to encourage manager Mel Machin to bring on substitute Imre Varadi by chanting his name.

Unfortunately, this mutated into chants of "Imre Banana" and that became his nickname.

The craze soon gathered momentum with City fans transforming the stadium into a sea of yellow fruit. Other clubs' supporters also got in on the act, most memorably

Above: A young Zara Phillips wearing a Barbour style raincoat and hat.

West Ham (inflatable hammers), Grimsby (fish) and Bury (black pudding!).

The highpoint – before they were inevitably banned – was undoubtedly City's visit to West Brom on 26 October 1988, when a variety of inflatables could be seen – sharks, penguins, even a swimming pool – culminating in a battle between Godzilla and Frankenstein's monster.

The Accused wins Jodie Foster an Oscar

One of the most controversial films of the year saw Jodie Foster playing a young woman who is gang-raped by three men in a public bar while the other patrons shout encouragement.

Based on a true story, *The Accused* was one of the first Hollywood films to actually tackle the issue of rape and Foster won the Best Actress

Oscar for her portrayal of Sarah Tobias. Kelly McGillis, a rape victim herself in real life, starred as the public prosecutor charged with bringing about justice who cuts a deal with the accused that so infuriates Foster that she launches a civil suit against the spectators.

Foster, born Alicia Christian Foster on 19 November 1962, started her acting career at the age of three for a television commercial, was nominated for an Oscar as Best Supporting Actress for her role in 1977's *Taxi Driver* and won her second Best Actress Oscar for *Silence Of The Lambs* (1991).

Above: Jodie Foster.
Below: Norwich City fans with their inflatable canaries.

1980 1981 1982 1983 1984 1985 1986 1987 **1988** 1989

MUSIC

April

1988 was a year of legal and personal strife for 'Godfather of Soul' James Brown. In April, he was charged with the attempted murder of his wife of eight years, Adrienne, who claimed that Brown fired shots at her while she was in a car and beat her up with an iron pipe, necessitating hospital treatment. Brown denied the charge. 'She is just mad because I won't take her on my South American tour,' he claimed.

A week later, Adrienne was arrested at Georgia airport for possession of the drug PCP (angel dust). She claimed to have been the victim of a set-up aimed at paying her back for the charges against her husband. (She died in 1996 after cosmetic surgery went wrong).

Brown had been arrested in 1987 for drugs offences for the fifth time in ten months. He was no stranger to jail, having been sentenced to eight to sixteen years for his part in armed robbery when he was sixteen. Brown served only three years, his early release being secured with the help of singer Bobby Byrd.

Ironically, the man whose many self-created nicknames included 'Soul Brother Number One', 'the Hardest Working Man in Show Business' and 'Mr Dynamite', was enjoying a resurgence in popularity in the mid to late 1980s after a dip in his fortunes during the disco era. The single 'Living in America' from the soundtrack of Sylvester Stallone's *Rocky IV* brought him to the attention of a new audience in 1985.

Following a high speed car chase with the police on the Interstate 120 in Augusta, Georgia, Brown was apprehended and, in December 1988, convicted of various offences including

threatening pedestrians with a firearm, abuse of PCP and failure to stop for the police. He served half of his six-year sentence and was released in 1991, immediately embarking on a comeback tour.

June

Post-Live Aid, charity and campaign projects proliferated with musicians becoming involved in many causes including Farm Aid, Red Wedge, Amnesty International's Conspiracy of Hope tour, the Ferry Aid single for the families of the victims of the Zeebrugge ferry disaster and Self Aid to raise money for the

Below: American singer James Brown at a press conference before his arrest.

REMEMBER THE EIGHTIES

featuring an all-star cast. The proceedings were broadcast live on BBC television, after initial cold feet by the politically-neutral corporation. Unlike Live Aid, the tribute was not a fundraiser, but rather an awareness-raising event to draw attention to the plight of Mandela who had been jailed for life in 1962 for opposing the white minority government in South Africa.

The architect of the tribute, musician turned activist Jerry Dammers, had inaugurated the awareness campaign with the Special AKA single, 'Nelson Mandela' back in 1984. He went on to found Artists Against Apartheid and it was the gigs he organised for that movement which led directly to the Mandela tribute.

Compèred by comedian Lenny Henry, the day included sets from Wet Wet Wet, Dire Straits (featuring special guest Eric Clapton), Eurythmics, George Michael, Sting, Whitney Houston (who sang with her mother Cissy), Stevie Wonder, UB40 (with Chrissie Hynde guesting) and the Bee Gees. Tracy Chapman performed twice, on the second occasion filling in for Stevie Wonder whilst he tried to locate

unemployed. The Nelson Mandela Seventieth Birthday Tribute Concert was heralded as 'the Live Aid of the late-1980s', resembling a rerun of the global jukebox, taking place on the familiar turf of Wembley Stadium on Saturday 11 June 1988 and

135

Above to below: Annie Lennox of the Eurythmics, Barry Gibb of the Bee Gees, Marti Pellow of Wet Wet Wet and Mark Knopfler of Dire Straits all performed at the Nelson Mandela concert.

1988

some missing, presumed stolen, synthesiser software. Chapman's debut album reportedly enjoyed 12,000 sales the following Monday.

Nelson Mandela was finally released from prison in 1990 and went on to become president of South Africa in 1994 in the country's first democratic elections.

July

House music originated in Chicago, as a combination of 1970s Philly disco mixed with drum machines and sound effects. It mutated into Acid House, characterised by a repetitive, trance-like beat overlaid with samples. The term was not initially drug-related, deriving either from 'acid burning' – Chicago slang for sampling – or from a song by Phuture, 'Acid Trax'. The

link with LSD, and its contemporary equivalent Ecstasy, came later when the use of both was prevalent amongst revellers at warehouse parties during 1988's Second Summer of Love.

The music arrived in Britain via Ibiza, with the look – shorts, t-shirt and bandana – representing a never-ending summer holiday. The omnipresent smiley face symbol was taken from DC's *Watchmen* comic book.

The tabloid press lambasted Acid House following the death of

Above: Clubbers dancing to House music in Ibiza.

a teenager on Ecstasy, prompting a police crackdown on warehouse parties which in turn gave birth to the phenomenon of raves in remote locations.

SPORT

Sandy Lyle takes the US Masters title

In the 1980s European golfers started to make their mark on the world scene like never before. Sandy Lyle was one who for a handful of years competed successfully at the highest level. In April 1988, he followed up his 1985 British Open

victory with a win in the US Masters, therefore making him the first Briton to wear the famous green jacket on the Augusta course.

Lyle had held the lead from the second round but many who had witnessed previous promising starts from European-grown players feared that he would eventually disappear back into the pack.

However, the Scotsman held his nerve and his game together arriving at the final hole needing a birdie to take the title. He eventually did it the hard way, driving straight into a bunker and chipping out still some 150 yards from the pin. Taking the bull by the horns he went for the flag and left himself an eight-footer, which he duly holed to record an historic triumph.

1980 1981 1982 1983 1984 1985 1986 1987 **1988** 1989

Above: Sandy Lyle is presented with the famous Green Jacket on winning The Masters.
Below: Lyle plays out of a bunker on his way to victory.

REMEMBER THE EIGHTIES

Holland claim European Football Championship

Nobody could have safely predicted the finalists in the European Football Championship played in West Germany during two weeks in June, for the two most likely teams to contest the final game had always looked likely to be the home country and Italy. Germany, managed by Franz Beckenbauer, had one of the most respected and talented teams in the world, including Völler and Klinsmann. Italy looked to be one of the improving sides approaching the tournament, sporting players like Vialli, Mancini and Maldini.

All looked to be going to plan, as both teams qualified for the semi-finals – but Holland and the Soviet Union were to upset the party. Holland scored two goals late in the game, from Marco Van Basten and

Ronald Koeman, to dispose of the hosts and Italy were downed by two second-half goals from Oleg Protasov and Sergiy Litovchenko.

Holland had been beaten by the Soviets 1-0 in their group game, indicating a close final was on the cards but with Ruud Gullit and Van Basten providing that extra bit of class, the men in orange ran out 2-0 winners. Gullit scored with a header and Van Basten connected with a wonderful volley for the other. The latter finished as leading scorer in the competition with five goals, to add to the seven he had bagged in helping Holland qualify.

England, the only home country taking part in the competition limited to eight teams, had an abject time amidst problems with hooligans. They lost their opening game to the Republic of Ireland 1-0, struggled in losing to Holland 3-1 and succumbed to the Soviet Union by the same score. The Irish side achieved a creditable

Below: Ruud Gullit of Holland with the European Championship trophy.

138

single gold caused questions to be asked. The usual suspects picked up silvers i.e. Linford Christie, Colin Jackson, Liz McColgan and the 4 x 100 metres relay team – but that, apart from a silver and couple of bronzes, was that.

Carl Lewis claimed two golds, thanks in part to Johnson's disqualification, Sergei Bubka, the metronomic pole-vaulter from the USSR, confirmed his position as the greatest ever and America's Jackie Joyner-Kersee set a new world record for the heptathlon.

Britain's total of five gold medals came courtesy of the men's hockey team, who beat West Germany in a pulsating final, Mike McIntyre and Bryn Vaile for star-class yachting, Steve Redgrave and Andy Holmes in rowing's coxless pairs, Malcolm Cooper for small-bore

draw against the Soviets but lost by the only goal of the game to Holland.

Seoul Olympic Games

Sports stories in 1988 did not come bigger than the stripping of Ben Johnson's Olympic 100 metres gold medal after he had failed a drug's test, but he was not alone. The taint of drug-taking hung over these games like a menacing cloud and placed into question so many other medal-winning performances. In total nine athletes were disqualified, including a member of the British judo team and even Florence Griffith-Joyner, who won three athletic gold medals for the USA, came under suspicion.

The scarcity of medals for Great Britain in the athletics was nothing new but the lack of a

Above: Drama as Ben Johnson seemingly wins Olympic gold in the 100m final.
Below: Flo-Jo wins the women's 100m.

rifle shooting and Adrian Moorhouse in the 100 metres breaststroke, one of only three medals won in the pool.

The swimming events had two star performers. In the men's it was the USA's Matt Biondi and the women had East Germany's Kristin Otto, both winning five gold medals. Boxing for once had no dominating force, the most interesting final coming in the super-heavyweight division where Lennox Lewis, flying the flag for Canada, defeated American Riddick Bowe.

POLITICS & CURRENT AFFAIRS

Turin Shroud a fake

Two weeks into October, a wringing of hands took place within the Catholic Church when the sacred relic known as 'The Turin Shroud' was declared a fake. Radiocarbon tests revealed the shroud dated from the fourteenth century, therefore dismissing any chances that the image of a crucified man could be that of Christ. Even the Cardinal of Turin, Anastasio Albert Ballestro, admitted it to being fake.

Since the sixteenth century, the bloodstained woven cloth measuring approximately 14 feet by 3.5 feet had long been regarded as the shroud

Above: Jackie Joyner-Kersee with the javelin on her way to heptathlon gold.
Below: Adrian Moorhouse celebrates victory after winning the 100m breaststroke.

REMEMBER THE EIGHTIES

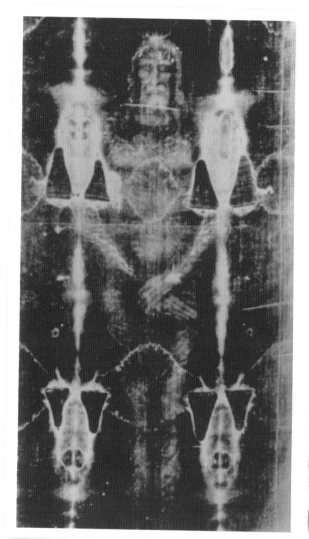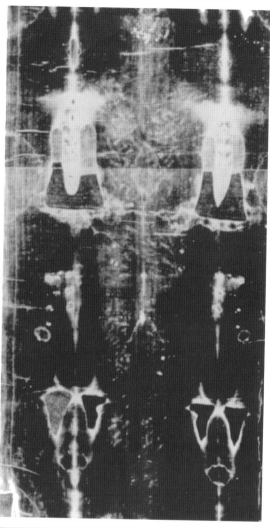

which had been wrapped around Christ after he had been taken from the cross. It had been repaired due to fire damage on more than one occasion after its existence had first been recorded in 1357. Although scepticism had always been rife, the Catholic world had long clung to the belief in its authenticity and had reason to do so.

Even more speculation materialised after the findings, many experts taking the 'I Told You So' route but that still did not explain the origins of the cloth and its imprint. The medieval fake theory was easy to accept, for such unoriginal relics were constantly being identified or unearthed.

In the twenty-first century doubts were cast upon the findings of the 1988 report. A man by the name of Raymond Rogers published a research paper which claimed the sample tested at Oxford University had been taken from a repair patch, coming from a much later period than the majority of the shroud. He did not rule out the possibility of the original shroud material being 2,000 to 3,000 years old.

The arguments rolled on!

George Bush elected

In November, the American vice-president George Bush took one step up the ladder and duly won the

Above: The Shroud of Turin.

1980 1981 1982 1983 1984 1985 1986 1987 1988 1989

presidential election. The Republican pairing of Bush and Dan Quayle took 54 per cent of the vote in defeating the Democratic hopefuls Michael Dukakis and Lloyd Bentsen.

Three months before the vote, Dukakis seemed to have it in the bag, as his main line of attack concentrated on the plight of the economy. But Bush Senior rallied strongly, the main tack of his campaign being his promise not to raise taxes. Although this promise would eventually be broken, it certainly served as a vote-winner.

Bush's problems were obvious from the start, one of his main obstacles being the Democratic majority in Congress but the thawing of East/West relations during his presidency, exemplified by the pulling down of the Berlin Wall, gave him a little easier ride on the international stage than many of his forerunners had.

The Lockerbie disaster

On the evening of 21 December, Pan Am Flight 103 crashed onto the Scottish Border town of Lockerbie, killing 259 who were on the Boeing 747 and 11 on the ground. 189 of the victims had come from the USA. The plane had been on its way from Frankfurt to New York and, after a stopover at Heathrow had resumed its journey at 6.25 p.m., only to disappear off the radar 44 minutes after take-off.

The aircraft had disintegrated in mid-air after an explosion and spread its remains over the Scottish town and surrounding countryside. The local emergency services had difficulty in coping and RAF helicopters flew in medical personnel to augment the effort. During the next 24 hours troops and policemen were drafted in to sift through the wreckage for any evidence that might give a clue as to what had caused Flight 103 to explode.

Below: George Bush.

softening, virtually served up two suspects on a plate. So-called intelligence agents Abdelbaset Ali Mohmed Al-Megrahi and Al Amin Khalifa Fhimah were charged with the crime of planting the explosive. The former was jailed for life in 2001, while the lack of evidence against the latter produced a not guilty verdict.

Al-Megrahi had an appeal turned down in 2002 but doubts about the verdict remained after suggestions of planted evidence were alluded to.

First signs that a bomb may have been involved, came when the US divulged that a number of their embassies had been issued a warning suggesting a Pan Am flight would be the likely target for terrorist bomb. The official investigation into the tragedy confirmed the theory and the search for the perpetrators began.

The finger of suspicion fell on Libya as the likely source of the bomb and, after some time, the Libyan leader General Gaddafi, whose attitudes to the West were

1980 1981 1982 1983 1984 1985 1986 1987 **1988** 1989

Above: The wreckage of the New York bound Boeing 747 that exploded over Lockerbie.
Below: The damage caused by the explosion.

1980 1981 1982 1983 1984 1985 1986 1987 1988 1989

1989

FASHION, CULTURE & ENTERTAINMENT

Sky TV

There was a cultural revolution in terms of British television on 5 February 1989 with the first broadcast of Sky Television from the Astra 1A satellite. Originally offering just Sky Channel – later renamed Sky One – Sky News, Sky Movies and Eurosport, viewers now had double the basic four terrestrial channels to choose from thanks to media tycoon Rupert Murdoch's venture – although some would still complain that there was nothing to watch!

The first television channel that had aired in the UK was BBC1 on 2 November 1936, with ITV following in 1955, BBC2 in 1964 and then Channel 4 on 2 November 1982 (Channel 5 finally arrived in March

Below: Rupert Murdoch, newspaper publisher and entrepreneur who owns Sky Television.

144

merged to form British Sky Broadcasting (BSkyB). BSB brought with it its own Movie Channel and Sports Channel – which became Sky Sports in 1991 – to offer an even wider choice to viewers.

The analogue service was phased out from 1998, ceasing completely three years later, as technological advances allowed the opportunity to broadcast hundreds of channels, and Sky Digital was born.

Baggies/Joe Bloggs jeans

The fashion for baggies – oversized jeans – had its roots in America where youngsters adopted the type of clothing worn by Chicano gangs in Los Angeles. (The term Chicano was originally insulting, but has since been adopted by those of Mexican descent).

Its arrival in the UK coincided with the explosion of grunge music and fashion popularised by such bands as Mudhoney, Pearl Jam and Nirvana and if you were anybody in 1989 you were wearing baggies and a T-shirt. One of the most popular was the Inspiral Carpets 'Cool As F**k' T-shirt and you only had to look at the latest music magazines to discover the latest trends and where to buy them. The baggies just *had* to be Joe Bloggs.

The Joe Bloggs Clothing company had been founded in the mid-1980s by Shami Ahmed, the son of a local retailer. His father, who had arrived in Britain from Pakistan as an aeronautical engineer in 1964, had opened Ahmed Hosiery in Manchester but soon realised that he needed to diversify. Shami was convinced that they needed a brand name and launched Joe Bloggs – so named because it was so impersonal that anybody could wear it.

The brand, offering designer jeans and trendy T-shirts, soon became a hit with the local youth and was publicised nationally by the likes of Manchester's boy band supergroup Take That who would wear the clothing in videos and onstage. All this helped Joe Bloggs

1997...if you were fortunate to live in an area that could actually receive the signal!).

Continental Europe had enjoyed the privilege of watching satellite television since 1982 but there had only been a limited availability as a cable service in the UK. With the arrival of Sky, satellite dishes began appearing on homes nationwide and the cable networks were soon being laid around the country with Cable & Wireless and NTL being two of the bigger providers. It was, however, estimated that only around 50,000 homes were able to watch the first broadcast because of a shortage of dishes to meet demand.

Murdoch's monopoly lasted just a year as British Satellite Broadcasting (BSB) launched its own service in March 1990 but by the end of that year the two rivals

Above: The Sky TV presentation backroom team.

1980 1981 1982 1983 1984 1985 1986 1987 1988 **1989**

1989 1988 1987 1986 1985 1984 1983 1982 1981 1980

Nintendo launches Game Boy

Computer games giant Nintendo launched its Game Boy system in 1989, a handheld portable device that is still in production in the twenty-first century. The pioneering portable games console had been the Microvision, which made its debut in 1979 but only survived for two years as it was easy to damage the keys and the early LCD (Liquid Crystal Display) screens were prone to leakage and darkening.

Nintendo, created in 1889 to produce cards to play the Japanese game Hanafuda, entered the video gaming market in 1977 and the Game Boy has since gone on to sell more than 200 million units.

become the first British jeans to enter the Top 10 and Shami Ahmed was a millionaire by the time he was 25.

Now with an estimated annual turnover of more than £50 million, Joe Bloggs offers toiletries and watches as well as the traditional jeans and Ahmed was named at number 13 in *The Telegraph*'s list of Top 20 Richest Asians in 2006.

The success of the Game Boy – with its black and green reflective LCD screen that prolonged battery life, directional and action buttons and powered by a Z80 processor – was heavily based on the game Tetris and children everywhere could soon be seen

Above: A model displays the grunge look.
Below: The Nintendo Gameboy.

on their travels trying to stack irregularly shaped blocks on top of each other.

Lambada look

Summertime is more often than not the time of the year when a new dance craze hits the floor and 1989 was no exception with the arrival of the Lambada. The term described both the rhythm – which originated in the Amazon – and the dance, incorporating other dancing styles such as samba, merengue, forró and maxixe.

The purveyors of the new sensual moves – dancing so close together that their stomachs were in contact, with their legs arched and moving from side to side – often wore distinctive clothing. The women bared their legs in tiny ra-ra skirts while the men strutted their stuff in Chino trousers and shirts unbuttoned to reveal their chests.

The popularity of the Lambada encouraged Hollywood movie moguls to cash in on the craze and films such as *The Forbidden Dance* and *Lambada*, starring a young Jennifer Lopez, were rushed out while the iron was still hot.

MUSIC

January

Various artists' compilations had been enjoying chart success since the 1970s when Arcade and K-Tel pioneered heavily-advertised budget price collections of the latest hits. The Virgin/EMI 'Now That's What I Call Music!' series began in 1983 with the first in the line reaching Number 1 at Christmas. By the end of 1989, the industry decided that compilations were taking up too many of the higher positions in the chart to the detriment of 'real' albums. A new spin-off Top 20 was therefore created for them in January 1989 which also included various artists soundtrack albums. This was the second recent change in chart arrangements; the announcement of the new Top 40 singles was shifted from Tuesday to Sunday in October 1987.

The first 'proper' album to benefit from the new arrangement was 'The Innocents' by Erasure, taking over at the top from 'Now That's What I Call Music! 13'.

1980 1981 1982 1983 1984 1985 1986 1987 1988 **1989**

Above: Erasure performing on stage.

1980 1981 1982 1983 1984 1985 1986 1987 1988 1989

September

A year of much activity for the Rolling Stones culminated in the release of the 'Steel Wheels' album in September and the start of the accompanying world tour. This was the first time that the Stones had worked together for three years and for a while it had looked as if the 'World's Greatest Rock and Roll Band' was no more. Mick Jagger and Keith Richards were at loggerheads, sniping at each other following Jagger's refusal to tour their previous LP 'Dirty Work'.

Lukewarm sales of the pair's most recent solo albums, Jagger's 1987 effort 'Primitive Cool' and Richards' 'Talk Is Cheap' from 1988, went a long way to convincing the Glimmer Twins that they could never match the commercial clout of the band on their own. 'It took all of that for him to realise we all need the Stones, that we need each other,' said Keith.

Jagger was blasé about resuming their working relationship after the acrimony. 'I just said "let's get on with it". I don't even remember half the things that were said.' The resulting sessions belied the band's reputation for slowness in the studio, as Jagger recalled. 'We just got on with it and wrote the songs very quickly as it turned out and recorded the album in three months, which is pretty good for any band – never mind one as ancient as the Stones.'

Above: The Stones on their 'Steel Wheels' tour.
Below: The Rolling Stones bassist Bill Wyman with his bride-to-be Mandy Smith.

speaking) model Katrina to front the group. Holloway was furious: 'Somebody else is getting the credit for my voice. I say Katrina is a phoney and she knows it.'

Black Box's UK label, Deconstruction, promised that the copyright holders, Salsoul, would be paid. Fearing legal action the group re-issued the single with Holloway's voice removed and replaced by a sound-alike session singer. The row highlighted the continuing uncertainties surrounding the still relatively new process of sampling. As the head of Deconstruction put it: 'Until a ruling is made one way or another, this will continue. You can't de-invent the sampling machine.'

November

The scene which became known as "Madchester", after a Happy Mondays EP released in November 1989, owed as much to Acid House and the burgeoning rave culture as it did to live rock music. The Haçienda nightclub, jointly owned by Factory Records and New Order, became the movement's focal point.

Happy Mondays, fronted by the era's poet laureate Shaun Ryder, encapsulated the new symbiosis of rock

The Steel Wheels tour morphed into Urban Jungle as it rumbled into the UK and Europe in 1990, breaking box-office records along the way. It was to be the band's last outing with original bassist Bill Wyman, 53, who showed that the Stones were not too old to cause outrage when he announced his engagement to 19-year-old Mandy Smith, whom he had been dating for six years...

October

Controversy surrounded Black Box's number one single 'Ride On Time' which was created by a three-man Italian production team. The song was built around an un-credited lead vocal sample taken from Loleatta Holloway's US disco hit 'Love Sensation'. Black Box recruited statuesque but non-singing (and non-English

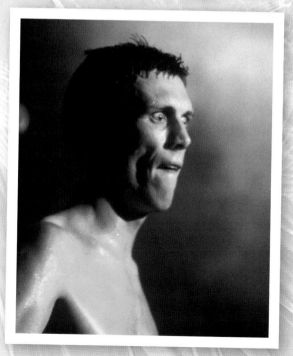

Below: Bez of the Happy Mondays.

– Inspiral Carpets, James and Northside – found themselves co-opted under the banner of Madchester.

The phenomenon was not entirely parochial; the city's fame spread worldwide with America's *Newsweek* magazine running a cover story on swinging Manchester. But, like so many youth cults before it, Madchester dissolved as it expanded. The Stone Roses drifted into a five-year hiatus between albums whilst the Happy Mondays' excessive drug intake led to a sorry end, bankrupting Factory Records in the process. Finally, following an increase in gang violence, the Haçienda was closed in 1997.

and dance. Equally important were the Stone Roses who, like the Mondays, had been around for several years before hitting their stride. The Roses' eponymous debut LP appeared in April 1989, almost without fanfare and initially failed to rise above 19 in the charts but quickly became a consistent feature in polls of the greatest albums ever made. To some, the record was too traditional, an accusation which could not be levelled against the single 'Fool's Gold', their zeitgeist-defining single, also from November 1989. The appearance of both bands on the same edition of *Top of the Pops* was a defining moment.

New Order weighed in with 'Technique', an album two years in the making, recorded in the Acid House capital of Ibiza. Other bands from the Manchester area

Above: Ian Brown, lead singer of the Stone Roses.
Below: Sugar Ray at the weigh-in before his bout against Roberto Duran.

SPORT

Sugar Ray Leonard's record earnings

After his fights with Roberto Duran and Thomas Hearns during 1989, Sugar Ray Leonard became the first professional boxer in history to make $100 million in fight purses alone.

Leonard actually fought in three separate decades, his career coming to an end in 1997 after an ill-conceived comeback aged 40.

But prior to this he had won world titles from welterweight to light-heavyweight, proving his ability to both play the role of the

consummate boxer or slug it out if he had to. During his time in the ring he retired three times, only to be lured back by his love of the sport.

Eye surgery interrupted his passage to superstardom but did not interfere in his most unlikely victory over the fearsome Marvin Hagler in 1987, when most pundits gave him little chance. The result may have been disputed; the records show he had defeated another boxing great.

1980 1981 1982 1983 1984 1985 1986 1987 1988 **1989**

Above: Sugar Ray Leonard fights Marvin Hagler during a bout at Caesar's Palace in Las Vegas.

REMEMBER THE EIGHTIES

1980 1981 1982 1983 1984 1985 1986 1987 1988 1989

Desert Orchid takes the Cheltenham Gold Cup

Within six years of his unpromising start as a novice hurdler, Desert Orchid confirmed his legendary status in the National Hunt world when the horse was the first grey to win the Cheltenham Gold Cup, before nearly 60,000 racegoers. On an unpromising day at the festival, with the ground heavy and racing around a left-handed track, which he never liked, 'Dessie' clawed his way back in the final furlong to defeat Yahoo by one-and-half lengths. The much loved steeplechaser had brought home the goods for his thousands of admirers and in the unsaddling enclosure three cheers rang out to acclaim his triumph.

His jockey Simon Sherwood had the most fulsome praise for his mount, citing his bravery and his ability to dig as deep as he could possibly go.

This win, over a distance way beyond his preferred two miles, proved to any lingering doubters that Desert Orchid was indeed a great horse whose two prior wins in the prestigious King George VI Chase, run annually at Kempton Park on Boxing Day, had been no fluke. After

fall in the 1991 race and retirement was bestowed upon him. His racing record was pretty impressive with 34 wins in 70 starts, the prize money involved being over £650,000.

In retirement, where he languishes in equine luxury, Desert Orchid's position as a charity fundraiser has been a highly successful one, for everybody wants to get a sight of a legend. Although no longer ridden, he has frequently been paraded in front of racegoers at major events.

The Hillsborough disaster

In April, the worst ever sporting disaster witnessed in Britain occurred in the FA Cup semi-final game between Liverpool and Nottingham Forest, played at Sheffield Wednesday's Hillsborough ground. The already packed Leppings Lane end of the ground saw

his Gold Cup success he recorded two further victories in the King George – a race difficult enough to win once, let alone four times, in 1989 and 1990.

Unfortunately, Dessie's attempt to win the race on a fifth occasion ended with a

an influx of further Liverpool supporters as a police officer ordered a gate to be opened to let fans in who were milling around outside in what he regarded as a dangerous fashion. This proved to be a fatal move, as this substantial number of people pressed in upon those present inside.

1989

Above and below: Desert Orchid is led towards the winners enclosure and then paraded in front of the crowd.

1989 1988 1987 1986 1985 1984 1983 1982 1981 1980

abandoned after six minutes, as the officials and players could not possibly continue in such an atmosphere.

The bodies of the dead and injured were passed over the fence onto the pitch, to be tended by the hard-pushed St John's Ambulance volunteers and a number of fans who also came to assist. The Nottingham Forest contingent, who had initially believed they were witnessing a pitch invasion, could only look on in horror as the tragedy unfolded. In the initial stages medical help was at a premium but eventually ambulances came onto the pitch which helped stabilise the situation.

In total, 96 people died as a result of the disaster, one living in a persistent vegetative state for four years, and 766 were injured. The Taylor Report which reported on Hillsborough, recommended that steel fences should be removed and all-seater stadiums be introduced. A positive from an horrific negative.

The ensuing mayhem found fans being crushed both on the terraces, on steps and in the entrance tunnel. The steel perimeter fence that was present at all grounds in the late-1980s to stop pitch invaders, proved to be a contributor to the carnage as young and old were pressed hopelessly against it. The game was

Above and below: Tributes are left in the aftermath of the disaster at Hillsborough.

POLITICS & CURRENT AFFAIRS

Khomeini death sentence on Rushdie

To moderate Westerners, the edict put out by Iranian leader Ayatollah Khomeini in which he ordered the extermination of London-based author Salman Rushdie seemed outrageously extreme. The February death sentence came as a result of the publication of *The Satanic Verses,* a Rushdie novel which dealt with sensitive issues involving fictional Muslim characters.

Khomeini declared the book to be blasphemous, prompting a march on the

British embassy in Tehran by a crowd chanting anti-Western slogans. In Pakistan, five people died during a hysterical rally condemning the book, Muslims worldwide felt they needed to make a gesture by burning the book in public.

Rushdie himself doubted whether many of those fierce Islamic critics had ever or would ever read the book, but the threat on his life had to be taken seriously by the police, who promptly whisked the author off to a safe location. The death threat hung over Rushdie's head for many years to come.

1980 1981 1982 1983 1984 1985 1986 1987 1988 **1989**

Above: Author Salman Rushdie, in hiding from death threats from Iran.
Below: Iranian religious and political leader Ayatollah Khomeini.

1980 1981 1982 1983 1984 1985 1986 1987 1988 1989

Tiananmen Square massacre

In an antidote to the relaxation employed by Communist governments in Europe, the Chinese authorities met fire with even greater fire in June when mercilessly cracking down on student-led protests that had centred on Bejing's Tiananmen Square.

Since the days of Mao Tse-Tung the Chinese leaders had never experienced organised questioning of their policies and history told us that toleration would soon turn into retribution. After all, any individual or group who had fallen foul of The Party in the past had been dealt with in an unceremonious fashion, often involving loss of life.

Armoured cars and tanks forced their way into the square, smashing holes through the barriers of burning buses, the barrage of stones and petrol bombs greeted

Below: A student cleans a plaque below the 'The Pillar of Shame' – a monument constructed to honour the dead and shame the Chinese government that refused to apologise for the Tiananmen Square massacre.

by hails of bullets coming via the heavy armour and foot soldiers. Unwisely, in an unequal contest, the students decided they had no alternative but to keep fighting rather than take to their heels.

The casualties began to grow by the minute, makeshift stretchers being employed by the students to rush their dead or dying colleagues to the overstretched hospitals. By the early hours of the morning, the rest of Beijing was in uproar, with fires springing up all over the city, but the Tiananmen protesters were finally quelled in a brutal, uncompromising final assault. Accurate casualty figures were hard to pin down but hundreds were killed, with thousands wounded, the balance between protesters and troops never apportioned.

The aftermath of the protest proved costly for even the most minor of dissidents in China, as a mass round up of individuals took place; they were then tried alongside students. The actions of the authorities were intended to send out a warning to any others foolhardy enough to believe they could confront hard-line policies.

Destruction of the Berlin Wall

As an almost inevitable result of the old Communist regimes in Eastern Europe losing their absolute power over the people, one of the great symbols of the East/West divide, the Berlin Wall, was breached on 9 November 1989 by thousands of residents from both sides as checkpoints were opened up to signal the end

Above: Tiananmen Square.

1980 1981 1982 1983 1984 1985 1986 1987 1988 **1989**

1988 1987 1986 1985 1984 1983 1982 1981 1980

of a divided Berlin. No longer would frustrated Berliners need papers to travel from one side of the city to the other, no longer would grim-faced Communist guards view everyone with suspicion. But most importantly, East Germans would now be free to move to the West.

The wall had been constructed in 1961 by the East German authorities who were alarmed at the constant tide of people moving to the western part of the city. After its erection, the wall became one of the most hated structures in the world, dividing Capitalism from Communism. No city in the world had such a pronounced demarcation line splitting the 'haves' from the 'have nots'. Around 80 East Berliners had died in their attempts to make it over the wall and escape to freedom.

The sight of unified Berliners standing on the now outdated edifice brought tears to many eyes and smiles to many faces as they chipped away at the masonry, either to hasten its

Above: A citizen of East Berlin peers through barbed wire at a West Berliner over the Berlin Wall.

destruction or simply to claim a souvenir. Fresh crossing points were soon being created for thousands of East Berliners, who only a month earlier had been part of huge protests directed at an already crumbling regime. Many of their countrymen had already departed East Germany via Hungary after that country had relaxed its border controls.

The unification of Germany must stand as a major event in the latter part of the twentieth century.

Purley rail crash

Less than six months after the Clapham rail disaster of December 1988 that claimed 35 lives near London's busiest station, another train collision occurred at Purley in Surrey, killing six and injuring 80 passengers. There should have been at least two and a half minutes between them.

The driver of the train that hit a stationary unit travelling from Horsham to London would later be jailed for four months for manslaughter after admitting passing a red signal, whereas Clapham had been caused by faulty signalling. Still, this re-opened calls for Automatic Train Protection (ATP) to be installed on all trains to stop them passing danger signals – a move whose cost was said to be prohibitive. Ten years on, a rail crash at Paddington killing 31 and injuring 400 would put the human cost of train safety back into the spotlight.

1980 1981 1982 1983 1984 1985 1986 1987 1988 **1989**

Above: West Berliners crowd in front of the Berlin Wall as they watch East German border guards demolishing a section of the wall.

Images Supplied Courtesy of:

GETTY IMAGES
101 Bayham Street, London NW1OAG

Concept and Art Direction:
Vanessa and Kevin Gardner

Design & Artwork:
Kevin Gardner

Picture Research:
Ellie Charleston

Publishers:
Vanessa Gardner & Jules Gammond

Edited by:
Michael Heatley

Written by:
Peter Gamble, Mike Gent, Ian Welch and Claire Welch